THE WEARABLE EDGE

Redefining Pharma Marketing in a Connected and Data-Driven World

THE WEARABLE EDGE

Redefining Pharma Marketing in a Connected and Data-Driven World

Subba Rao Chaganti

Pharma Med PRESS
An Imprint of BSP Books Pvt. Ltd.

™ **PharmaMed Press**

An imprint of BSP Books Pvt. Ltd.
4-4-309/316, Giriraj Lane,
Sultan Bazar, Hyderabad - 500 001.
Telangana, India.

The Wearable Edge: Redefining Pharma Marketing in a Connected and Data-Driven World
by Subba Rao Chaganti

Disclaimer: The authors and the publishers have taken due care to provide the authentic, reliable and up to date information related to the subject. However, neither the authors nor the publisher shall be responsible for any liability for any damage caused as a result of use of this book. The respective user must check the accuracy from other sources too.

Published by

™ **PharmaMed Press**

An imprint of BSP Books Pvt. Ltd.
4-4-309/316, Giriraj Lane, Sultan Bazar, Hyderabad - 500 001.
Telangana, India.
Phone: 040-23445688
E-mail: info@pharmamedpress.net
www.bspbooks.net/www.pharmamedpress.net

ISBN: 978-93-47311-30-7 (Paperback)

Disclaimer

This book is intended for educational, informational, and professional development purposes only.

While every effort has been made to ensure the accuracy, timeliness, and reliability of the content herein, the author and publisher make no representations or warranties with respect to the completeness or applicability of the information contained in this work. The case studies, examples, and references to companies, technologies, products, and regulatory policies are based on publicly available information and current practices at the time of writing. Some anecdotes have been adapted for narrative clarity, and any resemblance to real persons or proprietary strategies beyond what is publicly disclosed is purely coincidental.

This book does not constitute medical, legal, or regulatory advice, nor does it replace the guidance of qualified healthcare professionals, legal counsel, or official health authorities such as the FDA, EMA, or other governing bodies. Readers are advised to consult appropriate experts before making any decisions related to patient care, product development, marketing strategy, or technology deployment.

The views and opinions expressed in this book are solely those of the author and do not necessarily reflect those of any affiliated organizations, companies, or institutions.

All brand names, company references, and product mentions in this book are used solely for educational, analytical, or commentary purposes. They remain the property of their respective owners. No endorsement or affiliation is implied. The case studies and examples are derived from publicly available information and are intended to illustrate broader trends in digital health, wearable technologies, and pharmaceutical marketing. Every effort has been made to ensure accuracy and compliance with intellectual property norms.

The author and publisher disclaim any liability for any direct or indirect consequences arising from the use or interpretation of material presented in this book.

Acknowledgements

This book was born at the crossroads of science, storytelling, and strategic curiosity. I owe its existence to many minds and hearts that illuminated the path along the way.

To the scientists, engineers, data visionaries, and behavioral pioneers—past and present—whose breakthroughs pulse beneath every page: your tireless efforts to listen to the human body have redefined the future of medicine. From Edward Thorp's roulette-beating wearable to Rosalind Picard's affective computing, your stories shaped this narrative.

To the pharma brand managers, medical affairs leaders, digital health entrepreneurs, and AI scientists I've had the privilege of engaging with over the decades—thank you for your insights, your real-world case studies, and your belief that marketing, too, can serve healing.

To Anil Shah, Nikunjesh Shah, and the exceptional team at PharmaMed Press, who continue to support, polish, and publish my vision with care, professionalism, and a shared commitment to excellence—this book would not be in your hands without you.

To Naresh Davergave and his design team, whose visual sensibilities helped translate complex systems into accessible layouts—your work made the wearable world more readable.

To my beloved family—Mahalakshmi, my unwavering life partner, and our children and grandchildren, Srinivasa Phanindra, Geetha, Lavanya, Satya Shankara Aditya, Sowmya, Chaitanya, Aditi, Eesha, Surya, and Shriya—you are the rhythm that keeps my own heartbeat steady. Thank you for your love, your laughter, and your patient encouragement as I explored yet another uncharted frontier.

Finally, to the readers—fellow seekers, marketers, technologists, and caregivers—may this book help you not only understand the wearable edge, but stand at it with empathy, clarity, and courage.

Subba Rao Chaganti

Farmington, Connecticut.

Preface

There was a time, not so long ago, when the most a pharmaceutical marketer could hope for was to speak to a patient—through a poster, a prescription pad, a physician's words. The patient, in turn, was mostly passive. A receiver. A respondent. An endpoint.

Then came the digital wave—email campaigns, patient portals, branded websites, apps. Pharma began to listen. It learned to segment and target, to personalize and optimize. But even then, the relationship remained intermittent. Disconnected. Like a flashlight blinking in the dark.

And then—wearables.

Suddenly, patients were generating data by the second. Every heartbeat, every step, every skipped dose, every tremor, every night's sleep—or lack thereof—was becoming visible. Wearables took what was once hidden and made it continuous, contextual, and deeply personal. A steady stream of insight, not from a distant lab or occasional clinical visit, but from the lived reality of the patient's life.

This is not just a technological evolution. It is a philosophical one. A shift from episodic interventions to always-on relationships. From assumptions to insights. From generic messaging to empathetic presence.

This book was born from that shift.

It is not a manual, nor a pitch deck in disguise. It is a journey through the people, ideas, technologies, and breakthroughs that are fundamentally redefining how pharma engages with patients—and how patients are finally reclaiming their role as protagonists in their own care.

You will meet the scientists who first imagined computers worn on bodies, the engineers who miniaturized miracles, the marketers who dared to use biosignals to tailor interventions, and the patients whose stories, told through data, are changing how we understand adherence, behavior, and healing.

But more importantly, you will witness a pattern—one that will become clear as you move through each page: When pharma dares to listen not just with data but with empathy, when it stops broadcasting and starts conversing, when it shifts from product-centered to patient-centered thinking—the results are transformative.

This book was written for the curious marketer, the bold strategist, the ethical innovator, and above all, the listener. Because in the wearable age, success is no longer measured by what you say—but by how deeply you understand.

Welcome to the wearable edge.

Subba Rao Chaganti
Farmington, Connecticut.

Contents

PART II: THE INTERSECTION OF WEARABLES AND PHARMA

PART III: REAL-WORLD CASE STUDIES

APPENDICES

Introduction

When Technology Meets the Pulse

It begins, quite literally, with a beat.

Not the digital beat of a processor, nor the rhythmic hum of an algorithm at work—but the quiet, persistent thump of a human heart. Ancient. Primal. Unmistakably alive. For centuries, this beat was sacred and secret—hidden beneath skin, muscle, and bone. It was felt by healers, measured with stethoscopes, interpreted through intuition and touch.

Today, that beat lives in data.

It's captured by smartwatches, measured in milliseconds, visualized on dashboards, and analyzed by cloud systems running real-time machine learning models. What was once biological is now informational. The body has become a broadcast station—sending out signals that are increasingly readable, interpretable, and actionable.

This is where technology meets the pulse.

And when it does, something radical happens. Healthcare ceases to be episodic—it becomes continuous. Marketing ceases to be promotional—it becomes conversational. A person with a chronic condition is no longer a case number waiting for a follow-up, but a dynamic stream of insights—walking, breathing, interacting, deciding. And pharma? Pharma becomes not just a supplier of treatments, but a companion on the journey.

It's easy to think of wearable technology as clever gadgets strapped to wrists or stuck to skin. But that's like calling a telescope a tube with glass. The truth is far more profound. Wearables represent a tectonic shift—a redefinition of presence. They allow brands, researchers, physicians, and patients to meet not in a sterile clinic, but in the fluidity of daily life. In morning walks. In skipped steps. In trembling hands. In silent nights of insomnia.

In the pulse.

For the pharmaceutical marketer, this moment is both exhilarating and sobering. Never before has there been so much access—so much intimacy—with the real-world rhythms of human health. But with access comes responsibility. The responsibility to interpret without exploiting. To intervene without overwhelming. To understand before acting.

We are at the threshold of a new kind of engagement. One where the signals aren't just demographic or psychographic—they are physiological. One where campaigns don't just chase attention—they anticipate need. Where strategy doesn't end with segmentation—but begins with empathy.

The beat of this new era is steady, persistent, and growing louder. Pharma marketers who listen well will not only hear it—they will move with it.

Because when technology meets the pulse, it's not just data that comes alive.

It's trust. It's connection.

It's care.

The Wearable Edge: Skin Deep No More

In 2015, a man named Mark, fifty-seven years old and recently diagnosed with congestive heart failure, was given something unexpected—not a new drug, not a surgery, but a small, adhesive patch. Barely the size of a teabag, it looked more like a nicotine patch than a medical marvel. Mark was skeptical. He wasn't a "tech guy." He still wrote checks by hand.

But within days, the patch started telling a story.

His breathing pattern changed at night. His heart rate variability shifted. Subtle, almost invisible weight gain—just a pound or two—hinted at fluid retention. All of it was captured, analyzed, and flagged—before Mark even felt unwell. His doctor received a silent alert. A medication dose was adjusted. A hospitalization was prevented.

Mark never saw the signal. He never heard the algorithm. He never noticed the data flow that quietly circled back to his heart. But it happened. That was the moment Mark stopped being a patient in waiting, and became something else—a node in a living, breathing, digital ecosystem of care.

It was also the moment pharmaceutical marketing stopped being skin deep.

The Old Way

For decades, the human body was, for pharma, a black box. A place where drugs entered, and outcomes—measured weeks or months later—emerged. Marketers relied on population averages, proxy metrics, and market research focus groups. They segmented by age, income, geography. They launched messages. Measured recall. Tracked prescriptions.

But what they couldn't see—what they couldn't hear—was the rhythm of real life.

They didn't know that a newly diagnosed patient might feel anxiety not at diagnosis, but when the first side effect appeared in the middle of the night.

They didn't know that compliance dipped not on Day 30, but precisely when a routine was disrupted—travel, a family crisis, a moment of despair.

And they didn't know that the body was constantly whispering. It just didn't have a microphone.

The New Way

Wearable technology changed that.

Suddenly, the body wasn't mute. It had a voice. It sent signals—continuous, contextual, living data. And pharma marketers, for the first time, had the opportunity not just to respond, but to resonate. To move from campaign logic to biological logic. From marketing calendars to circadian rhythms.

But the implications go deeper.

Because wearables don't just generate data—they generate intimacy. There is a kind of trust in allowing a device to sit on your skin, to track your sweat, your sleep, your strain. And with that trust comes a new responsibility for marketers. The wearable era is not just about tech. It's about touch.

In Gladwellian terms, we are at a tipping point—the moment when cumulative micro-data becomes macro-truth. When behavior isn't just reported, it's anticipated. When personalization isn't aspirational—it's automatic.

And this changes everything:

How we design brand strategies.

How we measure value.

How we speak, listen, intervene, and support.

In short, wearables take pharma marketing from outside the body looking in, to inside the body looking forward.

The Question Beneath the Skin

But the real question is not what wearables do.

It's what they mean.

What does it mean when your target audience is no longer a demographic group, but a body in motion? What does it mean when engagement isn't measured in click-throughs, but in cortisol levels? When your campaign competes not with another brand, but with a moment of fatigue, or a spike in blood sugar?

And what happens to marketing when the person wearing the device is no longer passive—but empowered?

These are not just technical shifts. They are philosophical provocations. They force us to confront old assumptions: That the patient is a static endpoint. That marketers are message broadcasters. That the body is unknowable between visits.

Because now we know otherwise.

From Skin to Soul

This book is a journey through that knowing. Through the science, the stories, the stumbles, and the breakthroughs that define this new frontier—where biosensors shape brand strategies, where empathy is engineered, and where pharma discovers not just how to reach patients, but how to stay with them.

This is marketing that's no longer skin-deep.

This is marketing that listens to the pulse.

That moves with the breath.

That begins at the skin—and doesn't stop until it touches something deeper.

PART I: FOUNDATIONS OF THE WEARABLE REVOLUTION

Part I

Foundations of the Wearable Revolution

The Man who Wore His Mind

In 1984, on the streets of Toronto, a man could often be seen walking with a computer strapped to his back, wires running up to a small display hovering just in front of his eye, and a keyboard strapped across his chest. Children pointed. Adults stared. Some crossed the street.

He was, to most, a curiosity. A walking contradiction. A cyborg before Hollywood made cyborgs cool.

His name was Steve Mann. He was a graduate student. And he was, quite literally, wearing his mind.

Mann called it the WearComp—short for Wearable Computer. It allowed him to see information in real time, interact with digital overlays, even broadcast what he was seeing to remote servers. Long before smartphones, smart glasses, or the term "wearable tech" had entered the vocabulary, Steve Mann was already living in the world we're just beginning to enter.

But here's the thing: no one took him seriously. Not at first.

He was dismissed as eccentric. Overengineered. Even paranoid. After all, why would anyone need to walk around with a computer all the time?

And yet, within just two decades, the answer would become obvious.

Because today, millions of people wake up, strap on a device to their wrist, and check how they slept. They monitor their heart rate during a meeting. They count their steps during lunch. They check their oxygen levels after a jog. And increasingly—if you're in pharma—they interact with your brand not in a hospital, not in a pharmacy, but through that device.

That moment—that invisible handshake between body and brand—is not science fiction.

It's biology meeting bandwidth.

It's chemistry meeting code.

It's the foundation of the wearable revolution.

A Different Kind of Invention

We tend to think revolutions happen in laboratories, with loud proclamations and market launches. But many of the greatest shifts in history start quietly. With a wristwatch that vibrates. With a patch that pings a cloud server. With a cough recorded not in a clinic, but in a living room.

The revolution in wearables didn't begin with Apple or Fitbit. It began in pockets of eccentric innovation—scientists trying to measure skin temperature in real time, neurologists looking to capture tremors mid-motion, behavioral psychologists wondering if a person's breathing could predict emotional state.

It began with the idea that the body has a story to tell, and technology might be the pen.

Why this Part Matters

This part of the book—the Foundations—is not just a history lesson. It's a map of the terrain beneath our feet. Before we talk about wearable-powered marketing strategies, AI-driven patient journeys, or case studies with billion-dollar brands, we need to pause.

We need to understand what wearables really are?

How they evolved?

Who built them?

And why?

Because if we miss this, we'll think of wearables as just fancy gadgets—nice-to-haves, cool features, lifestyle accessories.

But the truth is far more profound.

Wearables are interfaces between our biology and the digital world. They are extensions of our cognition, proxies for our attention, sensors for our emotion. They blur the boundary between what is felt and what is known. And as they grow smaller, smarter, and more integrated—they don't just sit on the body.

They become part of the body.

And for pharmaceutical marketers, that changes everything.

A Revolution Hiding in Plain Sight

Steve Mann is still alive. He still wears his computers. But now, he's no longer the only one. In airports, conference rooms, yoga classes, and clinical trials—people everywhere are wearing technologies he once imagined. Only now, the world has caught up.

What once looked strange now looks inevitable.

That's the funny thing about revolutions. You often don't realize you're in one until you're too far in to turn back.

Welcome to the revolution.

Let's see how it began.

Chapter 1

The Birth of a Movement

In 1961, a man walked into a Las Vegas casino with a computer in his shoe.

His name was Edward O. Thorp, a mathematics professor with a fondness for blackjack and a sharp dislike for losing. He wasn't a gambler in the traditional sense. He was a problem-solver. A pattern-seeker. A man who looked at the roulette wheel and didn't see luck—he saw physics.

Thorp and his partner, Claude Shannon—yes, that Claude Shannon, the father of information theory—built what is widely considered the world's first wearable computer. It fit into a shoe and used toe taps to input variables—wheel speed, ball position—and output a prediction, via auditory cues, about where the roulette ball was likely to land.

It gave them a statistically significant edge.

It was, to put it mildly, a disruption.

The device was never discovered, but Thorp later revealed it in his writings. The casino never knew that the roulette table had been infiltrated—not by a cheater, but by the future.

That moment—when math entered the body, and probability was whispered to the ear—wasn't just the dawn of wearable tech.

It was the birth of a new kind of intelligence—intimate, invisible, embodied. And that's where this movement begins.

Not a Gadget. A Philosophy

When people think of wearables today, they think of smartwatches and fitness trackers. Of blinking screens and polished apps. But that's like thinking the printing press was just about the paper.

Wearables weren't born out of convenience. They were born out of necessity—the necessity to understand the world more deeply, in real time, and from the vantage point of the body itself.

Whether it was a roulette wheel or a heartbeat, the idea was the same: If we could measure it as it happened, we could change the outcome.

But to truly understand the wearable revolution, we need to go further back. Before the smart patch. Before the pedometer. Before Thorp's shoe-computer. Even before Claude Shannon's binary brilliance.

We need to visit Leonardo da Vinci.

Da Vinci's Pulse

Around 1490, Leonardo da Vinci began studying the pulse.

Not just in theory, but in rhythm. He watched as the wrist throbbed. He noticed how the beat changed with breath, with emotion, with fear. He described pulse as "the music of the heart." He even tried to build a water-timer to measure its frequency.

He didn't have electronics. He had intuition. But the insight was ahead of its time: The body is a signal system.

Leonardo didn't need a smartwatch to know that the body speaks. He just needed a pen, paper, and attention. He was the first to imagine that the pulse could become data, and he was right.

From War Machines to Wrist Machines

In the 1970s and 80s, engineers working on military technology began shrinking sensors meant for fighter jets—gyroscopes, altimeters, accelerometers—into chips that could fit into wearables.

What had once been used to guide missiles was now guiding movement—in human bodies.

NASA funded early bio-wearables for astronauts. The military experimented with biofeedback helmets. And slowly, the science trickled down to consumer life: heart rate monitors for athletes, glucose monitors for diabetics, sleep trackers for insomniacs.

But it wasn't just technology evolving.

It was perception.

People began to trust machines to interpret their bodies. They began to seek out metrics for performance, recovery, productivity—even mood.

The mirror was no longer enough. We wanted dashboards.

From Outer Signals to Inner Lives

Then came 2009. A small startup named Fitbit released its first device.

It didn't have a screen. It clipped to your waistband. It counted your steps. That was it. And yet, that humble pedometer did something radical: it gave people a number. A number that said: You moved. You lived. You showed up. 10,000 steps became a cultural benchmark. Not because it was scientifically precise—but because it was emotionally resonant. For the first time, people weren't just wearing technology. They were wearing proof.

Proof that they were trying. Proof that they were enough. Proof that they were, in their own small way, optimizing their lives.

This was the moment the wearable movement crossed over—from performance to identity.

The Silent Shift

Here's the curious thing about revolutions: they rarely announce themselves.

There were no protests. No manifestos. No sweeping policies or televised speeches.

Instead, it happened quietly.

A woman checking her heart rate after a stressful meeting.

A father seeing his oxygen levels dip during a flu.

A teenager tracking REM sleep and wondering why he felt so groggy.

And increasingly—doctors, pharma researchers, and brand managers tuning in.

Not to the patient's voice, but to their vitals.

Not to what was said, but to what was sensed.

The Body Becomes a Story

Today, we are awash in wearable data: heart rate variability, blood oxygen, skin temperature, electrodermal activity, tremor amplitude, gait speed, voice tone, sleep architecture, and more.

But this chapter is not about data.

It's about the moment when the body started to narrate its own story—in real time. And for pharma marketers, it was the beginning of a profound new challenge.

How do you speak to a person whose body already knows what it needs?

How do you build loyalty in a world where sensors offer feedback faster than campaigns?

How do you position a brand when the brand experience happens on the skin?

A Movement, Not a Trend

Wearables are not a trend. They are a movement—a philosophical migration from assumption to awareness, from retrospective care to real-time connection.

They represent a new intimacy between humans and machines. And for the pharmaceutical industry, they represent the most powerful listening device ever invented—not because of what they show, but because of what they let us hear.

The Historical Origins of Wearable Technology: From Eyeglasses and Hearing Aids to Fitness Trackers and Biosensors

The Origins: A History Worn Lightly

From Eyeglasses to Biosensors

In 13th-century Italy, somewhere in the scholarly backstreets of Pisa or Florence, a monk picked up two curved glass lenses, placed them inside a rudimentary wooden frame, and set them delicately on his nose.

He blinked. The world snapped into focus.

That moment—so quiet, so ordinary—was the invention of the first wearable technology: the eyeglass.

He wasn't a tech innovator. He wasn't trying to disrupt an industry. He simply wanted to keep reading.

But what he created was nothing less than a device that enhanced human capability—a tool that sat on the body, extended perception, and altered experience. In a very real sense, it was a primitive augmented reality.

And it changed everything.

The First Quiet Revolution

Eyeglasses weren't just a medical breakthrough. They were a democratic act. Suddenly, aging didn't mean obsolescence. Wisdom didn't have to fade with vision. The body's betrayal could be bypassed—gently, invisibly, and personally.

And yet, we don't think of eyeglasses as technology. They're too mundane. Too ubiquitous. They've become part of the face.

That, paradoxically, is their genius.

Because the most transformative wearables don't look like technology at all. They look like you.

The Echo That Listened

Fast forward to 1898. A man named Miller Reese Hutchison, an American inventor with a flair for acoustics, created the first portable electric hearing aid. It was large, clunky, and required a separate battery pack—but it worked. For the first time, sound could be amplified on the body.

It wasn't just about louder voices. It was about rejoining life—conversations, laughter, music.

The hearing aid did for sound what eyeglasses had done for sight. It restored access. It gave dignity. It allowed people to once again feel included in the symphony of the world.

And once again, the device became part of the person—not just functionally, but socially. To wear a hearing aid was to reclaim connection.

A Pattern Emerges

If you look closely, a pattern begins to appear. The earliest wearables were not about data. They were about restoration. They didn't track—they returned something that had been lost: sight, hearing, movement, independence.

That's the first myth we must challenge.

Wearables were never about novelty. They were about need.

They weren't toys for the curious. They were tools for the disconnected.

And every subsequent wearable—no matter how sophisticated—has followed that same impulse: not to decorate the body, but to understand it, enhance it, repair it, or extend it.

The Rise of the Metric Self

The shift came subtly—almost invisibly—in the late 20th century, when wearables went from restoring lost senses to measuring active ones.

Consider the pedometer.

It sounds simple, even quaint—a device that counts your steps. But the first modern pedometer, popularized in Japan in the 1960s, was given a name that would outlive its technology: "manpo-kei," meaning "10,000 steps meter."

The goal wasn't medical. It was motivational. It introduced the idea that movement could be quantified, and that number could be used to shape behavior.

Suddenly, wearables weren't just compensating for something missing. They were coaching, nudging, guiding.

The body had become a performance space.

And the wearable was its coach.

The Fitness Tracker Awakens

In 2009, the founders of Fitbit released their first tracker.

It did what pedometers had done for decades—but added something revolutionary: data feedback loops. It didn't just count steps—it made you care about them. It added dashboards, milestones, badges, social comparison, and behavioral nudges.

It gamified health.

It consumerized behavior change.

And it turned biological motion into digital emotion.

With that single leap, the wearable movement crossed a threshold: it went from being assistive to being aspirational.

No longer just for those who had lost something. Now, it was for anyone who wanted more—more energy, more discipline, more self-awareness.

The Skin Becomes the Screen

Then came the sensors.

Tiny. Invisible. Skin-deep, yet powerful.

Accelerometers. Optical heart rate monitors. Electrodermal activity trackers. Blood oxygen sensors. Skin temperature sensors. Even ECGs that could fit into a wristwatch.

The wearable stopped being a simple coach and started becoming a clinician. It could detect arrhythmias, predict seizures, flag dehydration, track recovery, monitor sleep phases, detect stress—all while sitting silently on your body.

The skin, once just a boundary, had become an interface.

We had arrived in the age of biosensors.

So What Does It Mean?

Let's return to the monk in 13th-century Pisa, squinting at a manuscript, slowly placing two lenses on his face. Or to the man in 1898, smiling faintly as a hearing aid lets him hear his daughter's voice. Or to the factory worker in 2024, whose smartwatch tells her to breathe before a panic attack she doesn't yet know is coming.

They are part of the same story.

A story not of gadgets, but of grace.

Not of machines, but of meaning.

Not of technology worn on the body, but of understanding carried inside it.

Wearable technology, at its core, is a human story—one told through lenses, sounds, steps, and signals.

And it's only just begun.

Key Milestones and Early Inventors

This is not a list of milestones. It's a story of human curiosity—how a painter, a gambler, and a cyborg helped shape the revolution we're all now wearing.

The Visionaries Who Wore the Future

If you were to trace the genealogy of wearable technology, it would not lead you first to Silicon Valley.

It would take you, instead, to a man with paint-stained fingers, dissecting cadavers by candlelight, trying to draw the invisible rhythm of life.

His name was Leonardo da Vinci.

And he may have drawn the world's first sketch of a heart monitor.

Leonardo: Drawing the Beat of Life

Leonardo was fascinated by the pulse—not just as a medical phenomenon, but as a language. He believed that every beat of the heart carried a message, that the pulse changed not only with exertion but with emotion, breath, and intention.

In one of his anatomical studies from the early 1500s, he proposed a device that could measure the volume of blood the heart pumped—centuries before the invention of modern hemodynamics. He imagined a vessel, shaped like an hourglass, designed to count the volume of blood displaced with each beat. Primitive, yes. But the idea was shockingly modern: a machine that sits quietly beside the body, recording its signals in real time.

Leonardo didn't call it a wearable, of course.

But he understood what few others did at the time: that the body was data, and that data could be measured, interpreted, even predicted.

He was, in effect, trying to map the music of the human machine.

Edward O. Thorp: The Shoe That Outsmarted Vegas

Four hundred years later, another man listened to rhythm—not of the heart, but of the roulette wheel.

In the early 1960s, Edward O. Thorp, a mathematics professor, teamed up with Claude Shannon, the father of information theory. Their goal was deceptively simple: beat the house.

They observed that a roulette ball, once spun, followed a physical trajectory—a predictable arc. With the right calculations and the right timing, you could predict the slot where the ball would land with a probability far higher than chance.

So they built a computer—small enough to fit in a shoe, controlled by toe taps, and wired to deliver discreet signals through a speaker concealed in the ear.

It was the first wearable computer.

It didn't monitor physiology. It didn't connect to a network. It didn't even have a screen. But it did something revolutionary: it took real-time inputs from the environment and translated them into action through the human body.

It was the beginning of cybernetic companionship—technology not used on people, but with them, intimately and invisibly.

Steve Mann: The Man Who Wore His Mind

In the 1980s, on the campus of MIT and later on the streets of Toronto, a graduate student began to attract attention—not for what he said, but for what he wore.

Steve Mann had built something called the WearComp—a computer that could be worn like clothing. The display sat just in front of his eye, over one lens. The computer itself was carried in a backpack. He looked like a cross between a soldier and a science experiment.

People laughed. Some were unnerved. But Steve Mann wasn't performing.

He was prototyping the future.

Mann believed that technology should not just sit on desks or in pockets. It should be worn. It should see what we see. It should augment our perception, correct our blind spots, and record our experiences.

In short, he believed that the boundary between human and machine should become porous.

Decades later, his work would influence the design of smart glasses, augmented reality systems, and heads-up displays. Today, his concepts are embedded in devices we casually strap to our wrists. But in the 1980s, he walked alone—a quiet visionary in a noisy world.

The Hidden Pattern

Here's what's fascinating: these three men—Leonardo, Thorp, and Mann—lived in entirely different centuries, worked in different fields, and never knew one another.

And yet, they were solving the same problem:

How do you bring technology closer to the human body—so close that it disappears, and in disappearing, empowers?

Leonardo wanted to reveal the invisible workings of the heart.

Thorp wanted to see what the eye couldn't track.

Mann wanted to give technology its own eyes, connected to ours.

They weren't just inventing tools.

They were inventing ways of being.

Wearing the Future

It's tempting to think of wearable technology as something modern—as born in the age of smartphones and app stores. But the truth is more poetic.

Wearables began as dreams.

Dreams of knowing ourselves more deeply.

Dreams of extending perception.

Dreams of making machines not colder, but closer.

That's the real legacy of Leonardo's pulse, Thorp's shoe, and Mann's lens.

They weren't building gadgets.

They were building intimacy.

And that, perhaps, is the most radical technology of all.

Chapter 2

Anatomy of a Wearable

The Story of a Tiny Light

In 2014, a young man in Chicago received a message from his wristwatch. It wasn't a text. It wasn't a call. It was something far quieter and far more urgent.

It said his heart rate was elevated. Very elevated. Dangerously elevated.

He wasn't exercising. He wasn't anxious. He felt… fine.

He walked to a nearby clinic, more curious than concerned. By the time they hooked him up to a proper ECG, his smartwatch's quiet whisper had turned into a clinical alarm: he was in the early stages of atrial fibrillation.

He had never felt a thing.

But the watch had.

All because of a tiny green light—the LED underneath his smartwatch, pulsing against his skin.

That light is where our story begins.

The Unseen Beneath the Skin

Most people never notice it—the soft green glow that pulses beneath their watch at night. But behind that glow is one of the great breakthroughs in miniaturized health monitoring: photoplethysmography, or PPG.

The concept is simple. Shine a light into the skin. Measure how much light bounces back. Blood absorbs green light differently depending on how fast it's flowing. More flow, less bounce. Less flow, more bounce. The variation gives you heart rate—and when you chart it over time, heart rhythm.

It's not magic. It's physiology + optics.

But here's the twist: the genius of PPG isn't the light.

It's the intimacy.

The fact that a sensor the size of a sesame seed can sit quietly on your wrist, capturing the rhythm of your life, without you noticing—that's what makes wearables so revolutionary. They turn passive bodies into active narrators. And they do it by being humble.

The Silent Engineers of Your Skin

Every wearable has five basic parts:

1. Sensors
2. Power
3. Connectivity
4. Processing
5. Design (Form Factor)

But they don't feel like parts. They feel like seamlessness. That's by design.

Let's deconstruct each—just briefly—before reconstructing what they mean.

Sensors: The Ears of the Wearable

Wearables are listeners. They listen through:

- Accelerometers – They detect motion. Are you walking? Sleeping? Falling? Twitching?
- Gyroscopes – They sense orientation. Are you tilting your wrist? Turning your head?
- Optical Sensors – That little green light, as we've seen, can reveal the heartbeat of fear, fatigue, or love.
- Temperature Sensors – Detecting fevers before you feel them.
- Electrodermal Sensors – Measuring sweat. Not because you're working out, but because stress leaves a trace on your skin.
- Electrical Sensors – ECGs from a fingertip. Brainwaves from a headband. Muscle activation from a patch.

A wearable is like a tiny orchestra conductor, tuning into the instruments of your body in real time.

But sensors are just the ears.

You still need a brain.

Processing: The Brain Behind the Glow

Inside that sleek casing is a chip—usually no larger than your thumbnail—doing something remarkable: interpreting your body in real time.

It takes noisy, analog signals and turns them into meaningful metrics:

"73 bpm."

"REM sleep: 2h 17m."

"Body battery: 58%."

But here's the catch: that chip doesn't just compute.

It learns.

Many modern wearables run machine learning models on-device. That means your wearable isn't just tracking you—it's learning you. Your unique baseline. Your rhythms. Your anomalies.

Your wearable knows when your stress is your normal, and when it's not.

It's like a friend who knows when you're faking the smile.

Power: The Price of Listening

The smallest part may be the most limiting: the battery.

A wearable is only as good as its invisibility. The moment you have to plug it in daily, adjust it, troubleshoot it—it stops being a second skin and becomes a second phone.

That's why battery engineering is the hidden frontier of wearable tech. Solar charging, thermoelectric charging (using your body heat!), kinetic charging—all are in play.

Because the less you think about the wearable, the more it can think about you.

Connectivity: The Pulse That Travels

Every whisper your body shares has to go somewhere—usually via Bluetooth, Wi-Fi, or cellular.

But it's not just about uploading your heart rate to the cloud.

It's about connecting dots—between you and your doctor, you and your coach, you and your future self.

Connectivity isn't just about signal. It's about shared meaning.

Your stress spike at 2:17 p.m. becomes a data point in a mental health dashboard. Your drop in movement over the weekend becomes a nudge from your therapist. Your elevated temperature during travel becomes a trigger for early flu detection in a population heat map.

Suddenly, your wearable isn't just listening to you—it's listening for others.

Design: The Trojan Horse of Health

Steve Mann's original WearComp was a backpack with wires coming out of his hat.

Today's Oura ring slips over your finger and tells you more about your nervous system than your doctor could ten years ago.

What changed?

Design.

Wearables have evolved into aesthetic allies. They don't just sit on the body—they blend with it. From watches to patches to textiles, wearables are becoming invisible healthcare.

And that, perhaps, is the secret sauce.

The best wearable isn't the one with the most features.

It's the one you forget you're wearing—until it reminds you who you are.

What's Really Being Worn?

So yes, we can talk about photodiodes and inertial sensors and PCB architecture. And they're all fascinating.

But if you zoom out, what you realize is this:

You're not just wearing a device.

You're wearing a mirror.

A real-time reflection of your behavior, your biology, your mood.

And in that mirror, you begin to see patterns.

And in those patterns, stories.

And in those stories, you.

That's the real anatomy of a wearable—not the circuits and casings, but the conversation it enables between your body and your awareness.

The body is speaking.

The wearable is listening.

Are we?

What Makes a Device "Wearable"?

The Tale of the Umbrella and the Eyeglass

In 1905, a British gentleman walking through the rain would have likely carried two things: a pocket watch and an umbrella.

The watch told him the time. The umbrella kept him dry.

One was hidden inside a vest pocket. The other, held like a sword, announced itself with every stride.

Now here's the curious part.

Today, we would call the pocket watch a wearable, and the umbrella, a tool.

Even though, by surface logic, both are portable, body-adjacent, and aid in daily function.

So what makes the difference?

Why is something on the body not automatically of the body?

That's where the definition of a wearable gets interesting.

Because the secret has nothing to do with straps, sensors, or circuitry.

It has everything to do with intimacy.

The Invisible Line

To be wearable, a device must cross an invisible threshold. It must stop being an object you use, and become a companion—something that learns you, adapts to you, and in some strange way, reflects you.

Take eyeglasses. They don't just help you see. After a while, they become part of how you see yourself. People say things like, "I look weird without my glasses." Not because of vanity—but because their identity has merged with the object.

That's the first sign of a true wearable: it disappears—not physically, but psychologically.

You don't wear it. You inhabit it.

Five Criteria, One Philosophy

Engineers often define wearables with a checklist:

1. It must be worn on the body.
2. It must sense something—biological, environmental, behavioral.
3. It must process or transmit that information in real time.
4. It must enable feedback, insight, or action.
5. It must be comfortable enough to blend into daily life.

But as a storyteller, I'd offer a sixth, more elusive requirement:

6. It must change how you experience being yourself.

A wearable doesn't just track your steps. It tells you when you're stuck.

It doesn't just measure sleep. It holds up a mirror to your fatigue.

It doesn't just detect heart rate. It senses the tension you haven't admitted yet.

In short: a wearable becomes a witness to your life.

The Difference Between Carrying and Wearing

Think of your smartphone. You carry it, but you don't wear it. It's reactive. You have to pull it out, unlock it, ask it to help.

But your smartwatch? That's different. It taps you gently. It vibrates when your heart races. It knows, sometimes before you do, that something's off.

You carry a phone.

You wear a question.

You live with an answer.

The Ultimate Wearable: The Wedding Ring

Now consider this.

The most iconic wearable in human history is not digital. It has no screen, no sensor, no connectivity.

It's a ring.

A band of metal. Unchanging. Unconnected. Unintelligent by today's standards.

And yet, it transmits meaning. It shapes behavior. It changes identity. It is always on, always near, always symbolic.

So maybe wearables were never about data.

Maybe they were always about intention.

What do we want to remember?

What do we want to monitor?

What do we want to be reminded of, silently, throughout the day?

The Boundary Keeps Moving

As we write this, researchers are embedding sensors into textiles, placing EEG monitors in headbands, turning contact lenses into glucose meters, and designing tattoos that change color based on blood chemistry.

So what makes something "wearable" isn't a box to check.

It's a relationship to the body,

a conversation with the self,

and a promise to make the invisible visible.

The best wearables are not devices.

They are mirrors that listen.

Sensors, Connectivity, UX Design, Data Integration, Interoperability

The Inner Life of Wearables

Sensors, Signals, and the Story They Tell

In 2009, a woman named Ellie began to notice something strange. Her elderly mother, Ruth, who lived alone in rural Oregon, wasn't answering calls as quickly. She seemed forgetful, more withdrawn.

Ellie lived two states away.

But one morning, she received a notification—not from her mother, but from her mother's wearable device. Her resting heart rate had spiked. Sleep had dropped. Activity levels had plummeted.

Ellie called. Ruth didn't answer.

That data, that quiet alert, triggered a chain reaction. A neighbor was sent to check. Ruth had suffered a mild stroke.

She recovered because the wearable saw what Ruth couldn't feel.

It all started with a sensor.

But it only worked because of something far more complex: a conversation between hardware, software, design, connectivity, and meaning.

Let's unravel that.

1. **Sensors: The Skin's Sixth Sense**

   The first time you realize your watch knows you're stressed, it feels like magic.

   But it's not.

   It's a sensor—often no bigger than a grain of rice—gently listening to your skin. Optical sensors detect blood flow. Electrodermal sensors pick up tiny changes in sweat gland activity. Accelerometers measure tremors and stillness. Gyroscopes detect micro-rotations.

   Each sensor on its own is a microscopic witness to your physiology.

   But here's the twist: sensors don't understand. They just observe.

They are the outliers of the wearable system—collecting rich, raw, unfiltered experiences that don't yet make sense.

They need help.

2. **Connectivity: Turning Whispers into Signals**

   Imagine a library full of unlabelled books. That's what sensor data is like without connectivity.

   Connectivity is what allows that sensor's observation to leave the body—to become signal. Bluetooth. Wi-Fi. Cellular. Each method a kind of messenger pigeon carrying your heartbeat to the cloud, or to your phone, or to a clinical dashboard on the other side of the world.

   It's how your fatigue, your skipped steps, your arrhythmia—go from moment to message.

   And yet, connectivity isn't always visible. It happens quietly. Seamlessly.

   That's the thing about wearables: the less you notice them working, the better they are. Connectivity is the nervous system of the wearable world—silent, constant, essential.

3. **UX Design: The Feeling of Being Understood**

   So far, we've talked about what the wearable collects and sends.

   But what about what it says back to you?

   That's where UX design steps in—not as decoration, but as translation.

   When your wearable tells you you've slept 4 hours and your readiness score is 61—it's not just giving you a number. It's offering a narrative.

   Design determines whether that narrative feels like encouragement or judgment. Whether it empowers or overwhelms.

   Do you swipe, tap, breathe, or ignore? Do you feel nudged or nagged?

   UX design is the tone of voice of your wearable. It's the difference between a doctor who lectures and a friend who listens.

   And when done well, it turns cold metrics into warm meaning.

4. **Data Integration: Seeing the Forest, Not Just the Leaves**

   Let's go back to Ruth.

   Her wearable didn't just track her heart rate. It saw her sleep change. Her movement slow. Her breathing alter.

It was only when these data streams were viewed together that the pattern emerged.

That's data integration: the ability to stitch together dozens of signals and find coherence. It's how the body becomes not a list of metrics, but a story.

In medicine, this is the difference between early intervention and late diagnosis.

In marketing, it's the difference between generic messaging and timely resonance.

In life, it's the difference between knowing and understanding.

5. **Interoperability: The Ability to Speak the Same Language**

Now imagine Ruth's heart rate data couldn't be read by her doctor because it came from a brand that wasn't "compatible."

That happens. A lot.

It's called data silos, and it's the enemy of progress.

Interoperability is the ability of different devices, systems, apps, and platforms to speak the same language, to share information without friction.

It's what allows your fitness app to talk to your medical record, your wearable to talk to your insurer, your digital pill to sync with your health portal.

It's the grammar of the connected body.

And without it, even the best technology is just a lonely voice in the dark.

The Deeper Point

So yes, a wearable is made up of sensors, connectivity, UX design, data integration, and interoperability.

But none of those—alone—make the wearable work.

What makes it work is the relationship.

Each part depends on the others.

Each part interprets the others.

Each part is meaningless without context.

Just like in any human interaction.

The Human Parallel

Think of how we listen to each other.

- Our senses collect input. (Sensor)
- Our nervous system sends it to our brain. (Connectivity)
- Our mind interprets it emotionally. (UX)
- We link it to memory and experience. (Integration)
- And we express it in language the other person can understand. (Interoperability)

In other words, the anatomy of a wearable is a metaphor for how we relate.

It's not a machine.

It's a mirror.

And sometimes, a translator.

The Four Forms of Knowing: Smartwatches, Smart Patches, Ingestibles, and Implantables

In the 1970s, an engineer named Larry B. had a problem.

His heart was skipping beats. Not metaphorically. Literally. He had arrhythmia—intermittent, unpredictable, and potentially fatal.

But the episodes never happened at the doctor's office. The ECG would come back normal. The story stayed buried inside his chest.

Until one day, he was offered a device. It was the size of a matchbox. It didn't look like much. But it listened.

Not occasionally. Not for 30 seconds. Not when scheduled.

It listened all the time.

They called it a Holter monitor—an early precursor to what today we might call a wearable.

It caught the skipped beat.

It saved his life.

And it marked the beginning of something quietly extraordinary: continuous care, delivered not in hospitals, but through devices that live with the body.

Today, we've gone far beyond the Holter monitor. Now we have smartwatches, smart patches, ingestibles, and implantables.

But the deeper story is this: each form doesn't just offer more technology—it offers a different way of knowing the human body.

Let's look at them—not as gadgets, but as epistemologies of the flesh.

1. **Smartwatches: The Outsider with a Front Row Seat**

   The smartwatch is the chronicler.

   It sits politely on your wrist, gathering signals from your pulse, your movement, your temperature, your stress. It's the health equivalent of the neighborhood watch—always observing, rarely interfering.

   It's an outside-in approach to insight. Optical sensors look through your skin. Accelerometers interpret your motion. Algorithms try to guess your mood, your fatigue, your fitness.

It's the polite guest at the table—curious, well-behaved, and always glancing sideways at your behavior.

But it also has limits.

The smartwatch can't always see inside. It knows when you're pacing, but not always why. It sees tremors, but not neurotransmitters. It tracks sleep stages, but not the quality of your dreams.

The smartwatch, like a journalist, is observant. But not invasive.

And for millions of people, that's precisely why they trust it.

2. **Smart Patches: The Body's Sticky Note**

   Then there are smart patches—thin, adhesive sensors placed directly on the skin.

   If smartwatches are bystanders, patches are collaborators.

   They sit closer. They commit. They don't just watch—they interface. They monitor sweat for glucose. They read interstitial fluid for electrolytes. They detect respiratory rate from subtle chest movements.

   Some can deliver medications—insulin, nicotine, chemotherapy agents—making them both observer and actor.

   A smart patch is like the undercover nurse—subtle, persistent, embedded.

   They're often used in clinical trials, post-op care, chronic disease monitoring. They don't ask for attention. They just listen. Quietly. Continuously.

   And when done right, you forget they're there.

   Which is, paradoxically, their greatest strength.

3. **Ingestibles: The Body as Narrator**

   Now consider this:

   What if the pill you swallow could report back?

   That's the premise of ingestibles—sensors embedded inside capsules that, once swallowed, activate in your digestive tract and transmit data.

   They track drug adherence, pH levels, core body temperature, even bleeding in the GI tract.

   Ingestibles are one-time guests in the body—but guests who go where no device has gone before.

They are designed for moments of truth:

- Did the patient take their medication?
- Is there internal bleeding?
- Is the capsule reaching the right part of the intestine?

Think of them as detectives with a short window—they investigate, report, dissolve, and disappear.

But their data can trigger seismic consequences: dosage changes, interventions, even hospitalizations avoided.

And in that brief passage through the body, they become the most honest of witnesses.

4. **Implantables: The Lifelong Whisperer**

And then, we have implantables—devices inserted beneath the skin, often into tissue, muscle, or directly into organs.

Pacemakers. Neurostimulators. Insulin pumps. Glucose sensors. Even chips designed to release medication over time.

If smartwatches are companions and patches are collaborators, implantables are cohabitants.

They don't just measure biology. They merge with it.

They offer inside-out knowing. Direct neural feedback. Electrochemical measurements. Stimulation of nerves. Even closed-loop systems that respond to the body before the brain is aware.

They are invisible, but irreplaceable.

And because they stay, they must be trusted. Which means they must be tested, regulated, encrypted, and designed with a covenant, not a contract.

An implantable doesn't just live in the body. It becomes part of the body's story.

So What Makes the Difference?

Same goal—insight.

Different approaches—proximity, permanence, perspective.

But the real difference lies in this:

Each device type offers a different intimacy contract.

- A smartwatch says: "I'll stay close, but not too close. I'll observe, but not interfere."
- A smart patch says: "I'll be quiet, invisible, committed—but only if you let me."
- An ingestible says: "Let me in, just once, and I'll tell you what's really going on."
- An implantable says: "Let's make this permanent. I'll protect you from the inside."

These are not tiers of technology. They're tiers of trust.

Each level asks a deeper question:

How close are you willing to let the machine come?

How much of your story are you willing to let it hear?

And how much control are you willing to give… in exchange for insight?

The Body's New Cartographers

In the end, smartwatches, patches, ingestibles, and implantables aren't just devices. They're cartographers of the human experience—each with its own vantage point, its own dialect, its own distance from the truth.

Some walk beside us.

Some cling to us.

Some pass through.

Some stay within.

And together, they form a mosaic—a 360-degree portrait of a body not just living, but narrating itself in real time.

That is the revolution of wearables.

It is not the gadget.

It is the listening.

Chapter 3

The Scientists behind the Sensors

This is not a mere list of inventors. It's a story of how a few brilliant misfits, outliers, and contrarians gave machines the ability to listen to the human body—and in doing so, redefined how medicine, marketing, and meaning are created.

How Empathy Became an Engineering Discipline?

In 1996, a computer at MIT was able to detect sadness.

Not in another machine. In a human being.

The person was sitting in a lab chair, wearing what looked like a headband with wires and sensors. Her face was calm. No tears. No visible frown.

But the computer knew. It had been trained to listen—not to words or expressions, but to skin conductivity.

The lead researcher was Rosalind Picard, a computer scientist with a strange idea:

"What if technology could learn to read emotion?"

Her students laughed. Some colleagues rolled their eyes. Computers didn't do feelings. That was philosophy. Or poetry.

Picard called her field Affective Computing.

Today, it's the foundation of everything from emotion-sensing wearables to mental health monitors to real-time stress detection in your fitness tracker.

But that wasn't the point.

The point was this:

Picard wasn't trying to make machines emotional.

She was trying to make machines empathetic.

The Shift from Computation to Compassion

We often think of engineers as cold and clinical. But the best sensor scientists are, paradoxically, listeners.

They don't just build devices. They ask:

"What does the body want to say that the person might not know how to express?"

That's a different kind of question. And it requires a different kind of scientist.

Let's meet a few.

1. **Rosalind Picard – The Emotion Whisperer:**

   Picard started at MIT's Media Lab with a radical thesis: emotions aren't noise. They're data.

   Her research showed that emotions leave traces—on the skin, in the pulse, in the way we move. She built sensors that could pick up those signals—tiny spikes in sweat, changes in heart rate variability—and trained computers to recognize emotional states.

   Her invention, the Empatica E4 wristband, is now utilized in epilepsy monitoring, autism research, and behavioral health applications.

   But what made Picard revolutionary wasn't the tech.

   It was the idea that wellness starts where language ends.

2. **Alex "Sandy" Pentland – The Social Physicist**

   Pentland didn't start with the body. He started with human interaction.

   He wanted to know: What happens between people when they talk? What invisible signals pass between them? Could those signals be measured?

   He built the Sociometric Badge—a wearable that measured tone of voice, gesture, proximity, speaking time. He discovered that communication patterns—not content—could predict everything from team performance to workplace burnout.

   His field? Social Physics.

   Pentland showed that wearable data wasn't just about health—it was about connection.

He taught machines to listen not just to the heartbeat, but to the rhythm of relationships.

3. **John Rogers – The Skin Scientist**

   Most electronics are hard, cold, and rectangular.

   John Rogers believed they could be soft, warm, and curved.

   He created epidermal electronics—sensors thinner than a Band-Aid, stretchable like skin, capable of measuring hydration, temperature, muscle activity, and more. His designs mimic the mechanics of human tissue.

   No batteries. No screens. Just circuits that breathe with the skin.

   What Rogers pioneered wasn't just wearable tech. It was invisible tech—devices that vanish into the body, not to control it, but to quietly learn from it.

4. **Gabi Tóth – The Biochemical Detective**

   In Budapest, a chemist named Gabi Tóth began studying how sweat could reveal secrets: glucose levels, stress hormones, lactate.

   To most people, sweat was a nuisance.

   To Tóth, it was a window into the bloodstream, one that didn't require needles.

   Her work laid the groundwork for sweat-sensing patches now being developed by companies like Eccrine Systems and L'Oréal's My Skin Track pH.

   Tóth wasn't just building sensors. She was decoding a language most people never thought to read.

5. **Babak Parviz – The Eye Engineer**

   While at Google X, Babak Parviz imagined a contact lens that could monitor glucose levels in tears. The media called it "Project Moonshot." The FDA called it "interesting but incomplete." The lens didn't make it to market.

   But Parviz had started something bigger: the microsensing movement—technology small enough to live inside the eye, the bloodstream, the breath.

Later, Parviz helped lead Amazon's secretive wearable projects, pushing toward devices that could understand your health, mood, and intent without ever needing to be told.

His guiding belief:

"The future of computing is about disappearing."

The Pattern Behind the People

What links these scientists?

They didn't just want to capture data.

They wanted to capture truth—especially the truths people couldn't say, wouldn't say, or didn't know how to say.

They listened where others ignored:

- In sweat.
- In movement.
- In silence.
- In presence.
- In the space between sentences.

They turned signals into stories.

And their stories became sensors.

The Quiet Revolutionaries

None of these scientists built a "viral" product. They didn't set out to disrupt markets. They weren't pitching investors on TikTok-optimized biosensor rings.

They were chasing a quieter goal:

To help technology understand the body not as a machine, but as a narrative.

To help patients, clinicians, marketers—even algorithms—listen better.

Because sometimes, your body knows something before you do.

And the right sensor, designed by the right kind of scientist, might just help you hear it.

Stories of Pioneers Like Rosalid Picard (Affective Computing), Heike Kamerlingh Onnes (Cyrogenics), and Newer AI-Health Innovators

The Empaths, the Frozen Atom, and the Rise of AI Healers

What Three Unlikely Innovators Tell Us About the Future of Feeling, Freezing, and Knowing.

In 1908, a Dutch physicist named Heike Kamerlingh Onnes stood in a cold, dimly lit laboratory in Leiden, the Netherlands. He was staring at a coil of wire submerged in liquid helium—so cold it was barely above absolute zero. What he saw next broke physics.

The wire's resistance vanished.

It conducted electricity with zero loss. Perfectly. Silently.

Onnes had just discovered superconductivity—and unknowingly, he had given birth to a new idea: that the colder you go, the clearer things become.

Half a century later, another scientist—this time a woman at MIT—would discover that the quieter the body gets, the more emotion it reveals.

Her name was Rosalind Picard, and like Onnes, she stumbled into a revolution by listening closely to something most people ignored.

Rosalind Picard and the Science of Invisible Feelings

Picard didn't start in psychology. She was a computer engineer, trained to think in code and logic. But she began to wonder: Why were our smartest machines still so socially dumb?

They could beat us at chess. But they couldn't tell when we were bored. Or angry. Or scared.

What if emotion wasn't noise? What if it was data?

She began attaching skin sensors to volunteers—devices that measured tiny electrical changes in their sweat glands, known as electrodermal activity. What she found startled her.

When people were feeling nothing on the outside—no tears, no shouting, no breakdowns—their bodies were screaming on the inside. Stress. Anxiety. Fear. Fatigue.

The body whispered. The sensors heard.

That was the birth of Affective Computing.

She didn't set out to build an emotion machine.

She set out to give machines empathy.

Her invention—the Empatica E4 wristband—is now used to predict seizures, monitor stress in children with autism, and even assess PTSD in veterans.

And her insight? That feelings leave physiological fingerprints, and the right technology can read them like a diary.

Heike Kamerlingh Onnes: The Man Who Froze the World to Hear Its Secrets

Now back to Onnes—a quiet man, brilliant, meticulous, almost monk-like in his obsession with cold.

His goal was simple: to understand the properties of matter at extreme temperatures. But what he found was something much more elegant.

When cooled to just a few degrees above absolute zero, certain materials stop resisting electricity. Not reduce. Stop.

The electrons glide through them without friction. Without noise. Without loss.

In a sense, Onnes had discovered purity.

Superconductors today power MRI machines, particle accelerators, and experimental quantum computers. But at its heart, his discovery was not about tech.

It was about removal.

When you subtract heat, you subtract distraction. And when you subtract distraction, the system speaks more clearly.

That's the paradox: to understand the world, sometimes you have to slow it to a whisper.

Just like Picard did, 80 years later—with the body's emotional heat.

The Bridge to AI Health Innovators

Fast-forward to now.

The questions have changed, but only slightly. Today, it's not just about emotion or conductivity. It's about prediction.

What if a machine could know you were about to get sick—before you did?

What if it could detect depression in your voice, Parkinson's in your gait, or pre-diabetes in your sleep pattern?

Enter the AI-health pioneers.

Suchi Saria – The Sepsis Seer

In a hospital ICU, time is everything.

Suchi Saria, a machine learning scientist from Johns Hopkins, created an AI system that scans electronic health records in real time and predicts who is at risk of sepsis—a life-threatening condition often missed until it's too late.

Her system—TREWS (Targeted Real-Time Early Warning Score)—can spot warning signs hours earlier than clinicians.

She didn't replace doctors.

She gave them foresight.

Just like Onnes removed heat to reveal clarity, Saria removed time—compressing it, so that patterns emerge before outcomes occur.

Ajay Royyuru – The Molecular Listener

At IBM, Ajay Royyuru led a team that asked a simple question with dizzying implications:

"Can we teach AI to understand disease… at the molecular level?"

Using machine learning, genomics, and protein modeling, Royyuru's group developed systems that can predict how a patient will respond to cancer drugs, or how mutations might change a virus before it spreads.

It's not guesswork.

It's the future arriving early, dressed in data.

Royyuru's machines don't just calculate. They listen to biology.

Like Picard, like Onnes—they found insight not in volume, but in precision.

The Pattern Beneath the Personalities

What links these pioneers—Rosalind Picard, Heike Onnes, and today's AI-health architects—is not their field, or their fame.

It's their attunement to subtlety.

- Picard listened to sweat.
- Onnes listened to electrons.
- Saria listened to health records.
- Royyuru listened to molecules.

They weren't louder than their peers.

They were quieter.

They noticed things most people missed.

They believed signals existed before symptoms.

And they built technologies to catch the whisper before the scream.

The Deeper Moral

In a world obsessed with noise—notifications, metrics, dashboards—the most meaningful advances often come from those who build listening devices.

Not devices that shout.

Not devices that diagnose.

But devices that tune in. Gently. Continuously. Empathetically.

That's what sensors are, at their best.

They are translations of quiet truths.

And the scientists behind them?

They're not just engineers.

They're interpreters of the invisible.

The Interdisciplinary Ecosystem—Biomedical Engineers, Data Scientists, Behavioral Psychologists

The Strange Collaboration That Built the Future

Biomedical Engineers, Data Scientists, Behavioral Psychologists—and the Secret Power of Crossing Borders

In 1943, at the height of World War II, a team of scientists in Pennsylvania gathered to work on something that had nothing to do with bombs or bullets.

They were studying fatigue.

Soldiers were crashing airplanes—not from enemy fire, but from mental overload. They were flying for too long, too stressed, too confused by the dials and flashing lights of their cockpits.

So the U.S. military did something unusual.

They brought in psychologists.

Not to analyze dreams, but to redesign dashboards. To figure out how the human brain interprets information under stress. To ask questions like:

"Where should this button go if a man has 1.5 seconds to find it with trembling fingers?"

That unlikely meeting—between pilots, engineers, and psychologists—quietly birthed a field now known as human factors engineering.

And it planted a seed.

That sometimes, the best solutions come not from deeper expertise, but from unexpected combinations.

Fast-forward to today's wearable technology revolution, and you'll find a similar story unfolding.

Because behind every smart patch, biosensor, and AI-driven dashboard is a strange and wonderful team: the biomedical engineer, the data scientist, and the behavioral psychologist.

And none of them could do this alone.

The Engineer: Making the Invisible, Measurable

Start with the biomedical engineer.

This is the person who looks at your skin and sees potential signal. Who designs circuits that stretch like tissue. Who can coax a heart rate from a wrist, or hydration levels from a bead of sweat.

They know that the body doesn't cooperate easily. It moves, it breathes, it gets hot and cold and wet. And yet they persist—trying to build devices that are less intrusive than a bandaid, but more insightful than a lab test.

They are, in essence, translators of biology into signal.

But they don't know what those signals mean—not really. Not in context. Not over time.

For that, you need someone else.

The Data Scientist: The Pattern Seer

Enter the data scientist—the code poet, the statistical sculptor.

To them, raw sensor data is like a language full of half-spoken thoughts. A spike here, a dip there. Useless on its own. But run it through the right algorithm—clean it, label it, model it—and patterns emerge.

Suddenly, steps become fatigue.

Heart rate becomes anxiety.

Skin conductivity becomes emotional dysregulation.

The data scientist doesn't just analyze. They listen at scale.

They tell you when 10,000 wearers all had stress peaks around 3 p.m. They notice the tiny tremor that shows up before every relapse. They write the model that predicts the panic attack before it hits.

But even they don't know why you didn't take your medication. Or why your sleep quality crashes every Friday.

For that, we need the third figure in our quiet triangle.

The Behavioral Psychologist: The Human Decoder

The behavioral psychologist is the only one asking:

"What does it feel like to be this person?"

They study rituals, triggers, habits. They know that forgetting to charge a wearable may not be a tech failure, but a motivation issue. That skipping medication might not be defiance, but shame. That heart rate alone is meaningless unless you know the story behind the spike.

They understand that we are irrational, emotional, beautifully inconsistent creatures.

And so they help shape interventions: Should the device nudge or notify? Should it offer encouragement or silence? Should it vibrate, light up, or wait?

They don't just want wearables that measure behavior.

They want wearables that change it.

Gently. Sustainably. Empathetically.

The Real Innovation: The Conversation Between Them

Each of these experts—engineer, scientist, psychologist—speaks a different language.

- The engineer speaks in circuits.
- The data scientist in code.
- The psychologist in stories.

And what makes wearable technology extraordinary is not that each discipline is excellent in isolation.

It's that they've learned to talk to each other.

The most powerful breakthroughs don't come from a new sensor, or a sharper algorithm. They come from moments like this:

The engineer says: "This patch can detect a 3% drop in skin temperature."

The data scientist says: "That correlates with a 12% increase in depression symptoms."

The psychologist says: "Then let's design a feature that encourages movement, not with guilt, but with kindness."

And that's how you build something that doesn't just work, but resonates.

Why it Matters for Pharma Marketing?

If you're in pharma marketing, this matters more than you might think.

Because the future isn't about products that talk.

It's about ecosystems that listen.

It's about messages timed to mood, education tuned to energy, support offered not after the crisis, but before it begins.

And those capabilities aren't built in silos.

They're built at the intersection—where engineers, scientists, and psychologists meet, collide, argue, empathize, and co-create.

It's messy.

But it's where the magic happens.

The Final Twist

We often assume innovation comes from the lone genius. But as history often reminds us, the real breakthroughs tend to come from what happens between people, not just within them.

The future of wearable technology won't be dominated by any one field.

It will be built—inch by inch, insight by insight—by interdisciplinary alliances.

Because understanding the human body isn't just a technical problem.

It's a human problem.

And no single expert can solve it alone.

PART II: THE INTERSECTION OF WEARABLES AND PHARMA

Part II

The Intersection of Wearables and Pharma

The Day Pharma Stopped Guessing

In 2017, a woman named Dana, age 47, walked out of her rheumatologist's office with two things.

One was a prescription for a biologic medication for rheumatoid arthritis.

The other was a smartwatch.

She didn't pay much attention to the watch at first. It had been offered as part of a pilot program by her pharma provider—voluntary, of course. "To monitor symptoms and help improve care," they said.

So she wore it.

At first, it counted steps and measured her heart rate. Then it asked her to log her pain, once a day. Then it noticed something she didn't: that her gait had subtly changed—half a second slower, slightly uneven.

Three days later, her wrist buzzed.

A message popped up:

"It may be time to talk to your doctor. Your movement suggests a flare may be developing."

It was right.

Medication was adjusted. Flare averted. No ER trip. No weeks of recovery. No spiral of missed work and side effects.

That was the moment Dana stopped being just a "patient."

She became a participant in her own treatment.

And that was also the moment pharma stopped guessing.

The End of "One-Size-Fits-All"

For most of its history, pharmaceutical marketing has been based on assumptions:

- Patients will take their meds.
- Doctors will follow the guidelines.
- Populations behave like the average.

And for the most part, this worked. Sort of.

But behind those averages were missed moments:

- The man who skips doses, but never admits it.
- The woman whose insomnia worsens after every injection.
- The child whose asthma flares up not from pollen, but from panic.

The problem wasn't the product.

The problem was the distance.

Between visits.

Between data points.

Between intention and action.

The Wearable Bridge

Wearables close that gap.

They take what used to be invisible—heart rate variability, movement, temperature, stress—and turn it into real-time insight.

And suddenly, pharma has access to something it never truly had before:

The patient's life between appointments.

That's the quiet revolution.

A flare doesn't begin in a hospital bed.

Non-adherence doesn't start in a pharmacy.

Disease progression isn't scheduled like a sales call.

It happens in the everyday: while walking the dog, climbing stairs, waking at 2 a.m.

And wearables are there for all of it.

A Different Kind of Data

But let's be clear: this is not just about having more data.

It's about having different data.

Continuous. Contextual. Physiological. Behavioral.

It's not a static survey or a lab test snapshot. It's a story, told over time, by the body itself.

- When the resting heart rate creeps upward.
- When the sleep efficiency drops.
- When daily steps fall, not dramatically, but consistently.

Each of these is a signal.

And signals, unlike statistics, speak in the present tense.

Why this Part Matters

This section of the book is about what happens when those signals meet science, strategy, and story.

It's about how pharmaceutical companies are beginning to rethink:

- Clinical trials not as events, but as living ecosystems.
- Adherence programs not as reminders, but as relationships.
- Marketing campaigns not as impressions, but as interventions.
- Product value not as efficacy alone, but as real-world experience.

You'll meet the companies doing it—Roche, Dexcom, Takeda, Novartis.

You'll see the experiments—some brilliant, some premature, all instructive.

And you'll hear from the people at the center—not just the scientists and strategists, but the patients themselves.

Because in this new era, patients aren't just receiving care.

They're generating it.

And pharma's job is no longer to speak louder—but to listen smarter.

Chapter 4

From Patients to Participants

The Day the Body Answered Back

In 2018, a 62-year-old man named George was enrolled in a clinical trial for heart failure medication. He took his pills dutifully. He filled out his symptom diary. He showed up for his check-ins like clockwork.

But something didn't feel right. Not to him—he felt fine.

To his watch.

Every night, his smartwatch showed lower oxygen saturation. His heart rate variability was dropping. He was walking fewer steps, sleeping less, moving less, laughing less.

The trial team didn't notice—because the trial protocol wasn't designed to see it.

But the wearable did.

Eventually, the system flagged him for a pre-symptomatic decline. Intervention followed. Hospitalization avoided. Life, extended.

Now here's the twist:

George never said anything.

But his body did.

And this time, the system was listening.

The Old Role: The Silent Patient

For much of modern medicine—and nearly all of pharmaceutical marketing—the patient has played a single role: receiver.

The doctor prescribes.

The brand informs.

The system nudges.

The patient?

Waits. Listens. Obeys. Or doesn't.

This model assumes that information flows one way: from expert to layperson, from trial protocol to subject, from brand to buyer.

Even our metaphors reveal the hierarchy:

"We educate the patient."

"We empower the patient."

"We engage the patient."

But rarely:

"We learn from the patient."

That, it turns out, is what wearables change.

The New Role: The Real-Time Collaborator

Because once a patient wears a device that continuously tracks their physiology, the flow of information reverses.

Now the patient is not just a receiver.

They are a data source. A signal generator. A real-world sensor node.

They're no longer being monitored at appointments. They are monitoring themselves, between them.

They're not just reporting symptoms. They're predicting them.

And most profoundly—they're not just being told what's working.

They're part of the process that determines it.

This is what it means to go from patient to participant.

The Participation Spectrum

Participation isn't binary.

It's a spectrum—and wearables stretch that spectrum further than we've ever gone before.

Let's look at three key shifts:

1. **From Reporting to Streaming**

   Old model: "How have you been feeling?"

   New model: "Let's check your dashboard."

   Wearables turn episodic memory into continuous measurement. They remove bias, forgetfulness, and the self-editing we all do.

   Now, the truth lives in the stream—not the story.

2. **From Adherence to Adaptation**

   In the traditional model, the gold standard was compliance. Did the patient take the pill on Day 14?

   But in the wearable world, we ask a better question:

   Why didn't they?

   Because now we can see the patterns:

   - Sleep was low the night before.
   - Heart rate was elevated.
   - Stress signals were high.

   The patient didn't forget.

   They hesitated.

   And now we know when, and possibly why.

   That's no longer adherence. That's adaptive understanding.

3. **From Feedback to Co-Design**

   Once patients see their own data—on apps, graphs, dashboards—they start asking better questions:

   "Why does my sleep spike before infusion?"

   "Why is my fatigue unrelated to exercise?"

   "Why does my heart rate dip only on weekends?"

   They're not just participating in treatment.

   They're co-designing care.

   They don't just wear the sensor.

   They become the scientist.

Marketing to a Moving Target

Now let's talk pharma.

This shift from passive to participatory changes everything about how pharmaceutical brands must think.

You're no longer marketing to a hypothetical persona named "RA Patient, Female, Age 50."

You're marketing to dynamic physiological states:

- Fluctuating fatigue.
- Momentary stress.
- Recovery windows.
- Behavioral momentum.

The message can't be static.

It must be contextual.

It must adapt to the body's timeline, not the brand calendar.

You're not launching campaigns.

You're launching conversations.

And the patient is not just the audience.

They're the co-author.

The New Currency: Trust, Not Attention

In traditional marketing, the currency is attention.

In wearable-powered pharma marketing, the currency becomes trust.

Because once a brand begins interacting with you based on your physiology—your breath, your sleep, your stress—you expect something more than relevance.

You expect respect.

And that's the fine line brands must now walk.

Wearables bring you closer to the patient than ever before.

But proximity without empathy feels like surveillance.

Participation without agency feels like manipulation.

To truly engage the participant-patient, pharma must earn their permission, not just their data.

The Final Shift

So here's the big idea:

The real promise of wearables isn't just early detection, or better adherence, or personalized marketing.

It's restoring the voice of the patient—not as an anecdote, not as a footnote, but as a source of truth.

It's making pharma not just a maker of medicine, but a partner in precision care.

Because when the patient becomes a participant,

Healing becomes a dialogue,

Marketing becomes a relationship,

And health becomes a shared story.

The Rise of Real-Time Patient-Generated Health Data (PGHD)

The Pulse that Spoke First

In 2013, a woman named Jasmine bought a fitness tracker. She wasn't sick. She wasn't training for a marathon. She was just curious.

She liked the little buzz it made when she hit 10,000 steps. She enjoyed seeing her sleep patterns. She even started logging her water intake, mostly out of habit.

What she didn't expect was for the device to notice something before she did.

Her resting heart rate began to climb—just slightly, over a few days. Then her sleep quality dropped. Then came the fatigue.

She thought it was just stress.

Her tracker disagreed.

It warned her of possible illness.

Two days later, she tested positive for the flu.

That's when something clicked.

For the first time in her life, Jasmine realized:

Her body had been speaking before her brain was ready to listen.

And her tracker had heard it.

This was not a diagnosis. Not a prescription. Not a doctor's order.

It was something quietly more profound: a moment of real-time, patient-generated health data.

The Great Inversion

In traditional healthcare, data flows one way.

- From clinician to chart.
- From lab to report.
- From expert to patient.

It's episodic. Delayed. Filtered.

It treats the body like a mystery to be decoded only when invited.

But with wearable technology, that sequence flips.

Now, the patient becomes the sensor.

And the body becomes the broadcaster.

Every step, every beat, every skipped night of sleep—it all becomes signal.

Not someday. Not when asked. But now.

That's the radical shift:

From "health records" to health streams.

From data about you… to data from you… to data by you.

From Static Charts to Dynamic Stories

In the old system, your blood pressure is recorded once at the clinic—maybe 120/80. That's your "reading."

But what if you've had three cups of coffee?

What if you're nervous?

What if you slept poorly last night or had a fight with your spouse?

One number.

One moment.

End of story.

Now imagine your smartwatch collects that same data every five minutes.

Suddenly, you're not a snapshot.

You're a timeline.

Trends emerge. Variability tells its own tale.

It's not the number that matters—it's the narrative it belongs to.

This is what patient-generated health data offers:

A longitudinal self-portrait, painted not in labs and codes, but in breaths, steps, and sighs.

The Democratization of Diagnosis

What makes PGHD powerful isn't just that it's real-time.

It's that it comes without permission.

Not in a rebellious way—but in a liberating one.

You don't need an appointment to track your own sleep.

You don't need a referral to notice your stress spikes every Sunday night.

You don't need a white coat to know when something's off.

For the first time, the patient becomes the analyst.

This doesn't mean replacing doctors.

It means augmenting them.

PGHD shifts power—not away from medicine, but toward shared authorship.

You don't just follow the treatment plan.

You co-write it.

What Pharma Missed?

Here's the twist.

For years, pharmaceutical companies invested billions in trials, claims, and campaigns—trying to understand how patients behave.

They hired agencies. Built personas. Conducted focus groups.

And all the while, the answer was already on the wrist.

Already in the patch.

Already on the skin.

The patient was already generating data—honest, unfiltered, moment-by-moment data.

But no one was listening.

The drug got smarter.

The marketing got louder.

But the body got ignored.

Until now.

The Big Reframe

PGHD isn't just about metrics.

It's about meaning.

It asks questions pharma never used to ask:

- How does this drug affect my mood?
- What happens to my sleep after injection?
- Do I move differently when I'm scared of a side effect?
- Do I open the pill bottle but still not swallow?

This is the nuance that can't be captured in a chart or recalled in a 90-day follow-up.

It lives in the present tense.

And that's where pharma marketing must now live too.

The Ethical Turn

But there's a shadow side.

Because PGHD is intimate. It's you, digitized.

- It knows when you're tired.
- It knows when you skip.
- It knows when you lie to yourself.

And if brands start using that data without transparency or empathy—what begins as insight can feel like surveillance.

The challenge, then, is not just technical. It's moral.

Pharma must become custodians of trust, not just curators of data.

Because the body may be willing to speak—but only to those who prove they're ready to listen kindly.

The Final Irony

Jasmine, the woman from the beginning, didn't buy her tracker to avoid the flu.

She bought it to feel seen.

That's the unspoken promise of PGHD—not just early detection or real-time alerts, but a quiet, continuous reminder that your body matters. That someone—somewhere—is paying attention.

And maybe, just maybe, that someone… is you.

The Quiet Rebranding of Care

Pharma's Transformation from Treatment Providers to Health Partners

In 1975, if you had high blood pressure, you saw your doctor, got a prescription, and hoped it worked.

You didn't get a follow-up text.

You didn't check your numbers at home.

You didn't wear a patch or a ring or a watch.

You just swallowed the pill and waited.

If it helped, you stayed on it. If it didn't, you came back months later and tried again.

The relationship between you and the pharmaceutical company?

Nonexistent.

The company made the drug.

Your doctor delivered it.

You consumed it.

Everyone stayed in their lane.

It was simple.

It was clean.

It was over.

But something subtle has happened in the last two decades—something so gradual we barely noticed, and yet so profound it has changed the very definition of what "pharma" is.

The industry has quietly gone from being a provider of treatments to becoming a partner in health.

And it begins with a shift so small, it looked like a footnote.

The Shift from Product to Presence

In the early 2000s, pharmaceutical companies began investing in disease awareness campaigns. Not just ads, but education. They launched websites. Published checklists. Started helplines. Supported patient groups.

It was easy to dismiss. Marketing dressed up as mission.

But something was changing.

These companies were no longer satisfied with being the answer.

They wanted to be in the question—to be there earlier, before the prescription pad came out. Before the diagnosis was made. Before the symptoms peaked.

They wanted to show up not just as vendors of molecules—but as guides through complexity.

This wasn't just about branding.

It was a reorientation of identity.

The Rise of Patient Services: A Trojan Horse?

At first, pharma's new identity came in the form of Patient Support Programs—reimbursement help, adherence reminders, co-pay cards, nurse hotlines.

To some, this seemed self-serving. Wasn't this just a clever way to keep people on the drug longer?

But inside these programs was a different truth:

People weren't just struggling with disease.

They were struggling with systems.

Forms. Costs. Stigma. Side effects. Forgetfulness.

And in those moments of frustration, the brand that called—not to sell, but to support—became something rare in healthcare:

A companion.

Not always trusted. Not always welcome. But present.

And that presence began to change expectations.

Enter the Wearables: The Feedback Loop Tightens

Then came the wearables.

Now, the data didn't come from the clinic—it came from the wrist, the chest, the skin. The patient became a living data stream.

And pharma—if it was listening—could offer more than pills.

It could offer real-time insight.

Personalized coaching.

Just-in-time nudges.

Suddenly, the company wasn't just involved in the moment of treatment. It was part of the trajectory of health.

If a person's sleep was dropping and their stress was rising, the brand could intervene—gently, quietly—with advice, reminders, connection.

This wasn't about selling more.

This was about being relevant when it mattered most.

From Episodic to Embedded

The old model of pharma was episodic:

- A symptom.
- A visit.
- A prescription.
- An ad on TV.

The new model is embedded:

- In your routines.
- In your recovery.
- In your decisions.
- In your life.

It's not that pharma became your doctor.

It's that it became your co-pilot.

The one who says, "You might want to take a walk today."

The one who notices, "Your tremor has increased slightly."

The one who offers, "Here's what other patients like you found helpful."

That's not a transaction.

That's a relationship.

The Branding You Don't See

In traditional marketing, the goal is visibility.

In modern pharma, the goal is reliability.

You may not see the brand, but you feel its presence:

- In the support call that gets your medication delivered.
- In the app that tracks your fatigue and gives you insight.
- In the chatbot that reminds you to hydrate during treatment.
- In the wearable alert that prompts you to breathe during a moment of rising panic.

This is branding not through message, but through experience.

Not through logos, but through loyalty.

The Real Story

And maybe this is the real story:

Pharma didn't change because it suddenly became noble.

It changed because the world demanded it.

Patients demanded voice.

Regulators demanded transparency.

Technology enabled continuity.

Data required responsibility.

So pharma evolved.

It didn't stop making drugs.

But it started making connections.

It started building touchpoints, not just touch-ups.

And in doing so, it stopped being just a treatment provider…

And started becoming a health partner.

Not perfectly. Not always gracefully.

But undeniably.

The Implications of Continuous Health Data Streams

The Stream That Never Sleeps

In 1924, a Dutch physiologist named Willem Einthoven performed what would become one of the first electrocardiograms—using a contraption the size of a refrigerator, and a wire strung between two poles like laundry on a line.

The patient had to sit perfectly still, their limbs submerged in saline buckets. The signal was faint. The results came hours later. But it worked. The heart's electrical rhythm—captured. Translated. Recorded.

It was a single moment.

A pulse on paper.

Today, your smartwatch takes the same reading while you're ordering coffee.

Except it doesn't do it once.

It does it hundreds of times a day.

While you walk.

While you sleep.

While you speak.

While you worry.

And it doesn't wait for you to feel something.

It simply watches.

It streams.

It never sleeps.

That's the difference between a snapshot and a stream.

And it changes everything.

The Old Way: Moment-Based Medicine

Traditional healthcare has always been based on moments.

- The moment you feel pain.

- The moment you visit the clinic.
- The moment your numbers are measured.
- The moment a decision is made.

Everything revolves around events.

You get sick, you seek care. You describe symptoms, someone records them. Data exists only because of crisis or checkup.

The body, meanwhile, continues to operate in silence.

Unmeasured.

Unnoticed.

Moments are what we call punctuated knowledge.

The question is: What happens in the space between those dots?

That's where continuous health data begins to matter.

The Stream Arrives

With the rise of wearables, biosensors, and ambient monitoring, health is no longer a file in a cabinet.

It's a live feed.

- Your stress is a waveform.
- Your recovery is a trendline.
- Your fatigue is a time series.

You're not just being tracked.

You're being understood over time.

And here's the twist: the most important information often isn't the data point itself.

It's the change.

The drift. The deviation. The nudge away from baseline.

That's the whisper before the symptom. The tremor before the fall. The silence before the spiral.

In a stream, subtlety becomes signal.

The Disappearance of the "Normal Patient"

Once you have continuous data, the idea of "normal" dissolves.

There's no average heart rate.

There's your heart rate on Tuesdays, after skipping breakfast, during allergy season.

There's your version of fatigue—not as defined by surveys, but as seen in your steps, your speech, your sleep.

Continuous data tells us what's normal for you.

And suddenly, the idea of treating everyone the same—same dose, same schedule, same campaign—starts to feel like a relic.

Pharma must now speak not to populations, but to patterns.

Not to personas, but to personal baselines.

And marketing must follow suit—not in tone, but in timing.

Because when the body lives in a stream, messages that arrive too early feel irrelevant.

And those that arrive too late feel impersonal.

The Predictive Turn

The most profound implication of health streams is not observation.

It's prediction.

If your resting heart rate rises steadily for three days, and your sleep efficiency drops by 20%, and your skin temperature increases half a degree, the stream doesn't just say: you're sick.

It says:

You might be sick… soon.

This isn't science fiction. It's already happening in pilot studies across chronic disease, oncology, mental health.

The result?

Preventive care becomes preemptive care.

And pharma's role shifts again—from intervention to anticipation.

The Burden of Knowing

But there's a darker current in the stream.

When you see your health data 24/7, you also see:

- The bad nights.
- The skipped doses.
- The silent spikes.

Continuous data removes plausible deniability.

You can no longer say "I didn't know."

And neither can your provider.

Or your brand.

With great insight comes a quiet burden:

Once the signal exists, ignoring it becomes a choice.

This changes the ethical equation for marketers, clinicians, and designers.

What should you act on?

What must you disclose?

When does nudging cross into intrusion?

The stream doesn't just bring data.

It brings responsibility.

The Final Transformation: From Passive to Participatory

In a snapshot world, health is something that happens to you.

In a streaming world, health becomes something you're in dialogue with.

You don't just get feedback.

You adapt. You experiment. You notice.

It's the return of the embodied self—not through intuition alone, but through biofeedback.

Your body speaks.

Your wearable translates.

You respond.

This is not monitoring.

It's collaboration.

And once that loop begins, pharma, too, must learn to speak in the language of fluid, contextual presence.

Not loud. Not scripted.

But aware.

The Future Whisper

We are entering a world where silence is suspicious.

Where absence of data feels like absence of care.

In such a world, the most powerful thing a pharma brand can do may not be to interrupt the stream…

…but to flow alongside it.

To become a current in the current.

A voice not shouting, but showing up.

At just the right moment.

With just the right insight.

And just enough trust.

Because in the age of continuous health data, it's not what you know.

It's how—and when—you listen.

Chapter 5

Beyond the Pill

Wearables as Therapeutics

In 2016, a boy named Caleb was diagnosed with asthma.

His parents were careful. They followed the medication schedule. They used the inhaler correctly. They avoided triggers.

And yet, the attacks kept coming.

Until one day, his doctor handed him something new: a small, plastic sensor that clipped to his inhaler. It looked like a toy.

But it was anything but trivial.

The sensor tracked each puff—time, location, frequency. It synced with an app. It mapped his inhaler use onto city air data, pollen counts, humidity levels.

Within a few weeks, a pattern emerged:

Caleb's asthma flared not randomly, but almost exclusively near a specific intersection on the way to school.

That intersection had unusually high levels of diesel emissions.

The family changed their route.

The attacks stopped.

No new drug.

No new dose.

Just new data.

Delivered not in a pill bottle, but in a wearable therapeutic system.

The Pill as a Beginning, Not an End

Pharmaceuticals have always followed a linear path:

Discover molecule.

- Prove efficacy.
- Deliver dose.
- Wait for response.

The model assumes that the pill is the solution. That the therapeutic effect lives entirely inside a compound.

But what if the pill is only half the story?

What if the other half lives in the context—the air you breathe, the time you dose, the stress you feel, the sleep you get, the gait you walk?

That's what wearables are beginning to reveal.

They don't replace the pill.

They complete it.

Therapy in Real Time

The term "wearable therapeutic" sounds clinical, even cold. But it points to a simple, human idea:

What if the treatment could travel with you?

Unlike traditional medications, wearables don't wait passively in the bloodstream.

They adjust.

They prompt.

They respond.

Consider these examples:

- A smart patch detects rising glucose and releases insulin before symptoms emerge.
- A neurostimulator senses tremor onset and counters it with pulses—in the moment, not after.
- A wristband senses stress patterns and delivers real-time breathing cues or haptic feedback to preempt panic.

This isn't compliance.

This is conversation.

The Body as a Feedback Loop

In the traditional model, you take a medication and wait.

In the wearable model, you enter a loop:

1. Sense – The device detects something.
2. Interpret – Algorithms recognize a pattern.
3. Intervene – A vibration, a signal, a release, a reminder.
4. Re-measure – Did it help?
5. Adjust – If not, try again.

It's not treatment as a noun.

It's treating as a verb.

And what emerges is something radical: a therapy that is alive, learning from you, with you, in real time.

Marketing the Invisible Molecule

Here's the interesting part for pharma marketers.

You're no longer just marketing the pill.

You're marketing an ecosystem.

- A drug that pairs with a sensor.
- A wearable that tracks, nudges, or delivers.
- An app that visualizes.
- A feedback loop that builds trust.

It's no longer "our product reduces inflammation."

It's "our platform understands your rhythms."

It's no longer about efficacy in trials.

It's about experience in life.

You're not just claiming effectiveness.

You're demonstrating it—daily, passively, personally.

The Regulatory Riddle

Of course, not everyone is ready.

Regulators still ask:

"What is the therapeutic agent here—the molecule or the machine?"

The answer, increasingly, is both.

But that means wearables must go through the same rigor as drugs:

- Clinical validation.
- Safety standards.
- Privacy controls.

A misfiring sensor isn't just a tech glitch.

It's a failed treatment.

The stakes are higher.

And the opportunity? Even more so.

The New Therapeutic Contract

When you swallow a pill, you place your trust in chemistry.

When you wear a therapeutic, you place your trust in intelligence—how it senses, adapts, and responds.

This redefines not just treatment, but relationship.

You're not just "on" therapy.

You're in relationship with it—moment to moment, data point to data point.

And pharma's role evolves again:

From product-maker… to pattern-listener… to co-navigator.

Back to Caleb

Remember Caleb, the boy with asthma?

That clip-on sensor didn't deliver a drug.

It delivered insight.

It changed behavior.

It prevented harm.

That's a therapeutic too.

In a world where the body speaks in pulses and patterns, treatment may no longer be just what we give, but what we understand—and respond to—in time.

Welcome to the era of wearables as therapeutics.

Not supplements to care.

But partners in healing.

Not the future.

Already here.

Digital Therapeutics, Companion Wearables, and the Drug-Device Convergence

In 2017, the FDA did something it had never done before.

It approved a pill with a sensor inside.

The pill was aripiprazole, used to treat schizophrenia and bipolar disorder. The sensor—made of copper, magnesium, and silicon—was no larger than a grain of sand. Once swallowed, it sent a signal to a patch worn on the patient's torso. That patch then relayed the data to a mobile app. The patient, the caregiver, even the psychiatrist could see it: yes, the dose was taken.

The product was called Abilify MyCite.

But the real story wasn't the pill.

It was the moment the boundary blurred—between drug and device, molecule and machine, biology and data.

This wasn't medication.

This was a conversation.

And it signaled something profound: the disappearance of the line between what we take, what we wear, and how we heal.

The Companion That Watches

Imagine your heart skipping a beat at 3:27 p.m.

Not a metaphorical flutter—but a literal, electrical irregularity.

You don't feel it.

You don't call anyone.

But your smartwatch does.

It records the event. Flags it. Sends a report. Suggests you book a cardiologist visit.

Here's the twist: you haven't taken a pill.

You haven't seen a doctor.

You haven't done anything.

And yet, something therapeutic has occurred.

You've moved from unawareness to awareness.

From passive to participatory.

And that might be enough to save your life.

That's the premise behind digital therapeutics:

Not treating with chemicals, but with code.

Not altering your cells, but shaping your behavior.

A CBT app that reduces depressive episodes.

A breathing tool that helps with anxiety.

A gamified regimen that improves adherence in kids with ADHD.

It's therapy—just not the kind that comes in blister packs.

The Rise of the Companion

Historically, medications have been loners.

You take a tablet, and that's it. The drug does its job. You're not expected to interact with it, question it, observe it.

But companion wearables have changed that dynamic entirely.

They are:

- Watchdogs – tracking adherence, sleep, vitals.
- Coaches – nudging behavior, reminding, celebrating milestones.
- Translators – turning raw biology into understandable trends.

Think of them like a Fitbit that speaks fluent pharmacology.

Imagine:

- A blood pressure med paired with a wearable that senses sodium spikes.
- A diabetes injectable tied to a glucose monitor that adjusts dose recommendations in real time.
- An oncology drug linked with a wearable that tracks fatigue, temperature, and mood—helping triage patients before a crisis hits.

The pill no longer stands alone.

It has a digital companion.

And that changes how we define efficacy, compliance, even care.

When Molecules Meet Microchips

Now let's take it one step further.

Not just a drug with a wearable companion.

But a drug and device fused into one.

This is drug-device convergence—the tight coupling of pharmacologic action and engineered delivery or feedback.

Examples?

- Ingestibles that activate only under specific pH or temperature conditions, detected by internal sensors.
- Implantables that release pain medication in response to biometric stress signals.
- Smart patches that sense blood chemistry and deliver microdoses through the skin, tuned to real-time needs.

It's not one-size-fits-all.

It's moment-size-fits-you.

And here's the kicker: the more seamless the integration, the more invisible it becomes.

So we move from medications we take to systems we live inside.

The Software as a Drug

The FDA now recognizes something it once would have found implausible:

Software can be a treatment.

In fact, there's an entire category—"Software as a Medical Device (SaMD)"—approved for everything from insomnia to opioid use disorder.

That changes the game for pharma marketers.

You're no longer promoting a product.

You're introducing a partnership—between human and algorithm, between pill and pattern, between biology and behavior.

The value isn't just in what's prescribed.

It's in what's observed, adjusted, predicted, and learned.

The Behavior Behind the Biology

Here's what makes all this so powerful—and so human.

Most chronic diseases don't need new miracle molecules.

They need sustained behavior change:

Regular meds.

Diet.

Exercise.

Sleep.

Mental well-being.

Digital therapeutics and companion wearables don't just monitor that behavior.

They shape it.

And they do so without judgment—just gentle persistence.

Like a whisper at your wrist.

Or a light nudge from your phone.

Or a dashboard that shows: you're doing better than yesterday.

That's not gimmickry.

That's designing for accountability with empathy.

And that's medicine, too.

From Pillbox to Platform

As pharma shifts into this new era, its identity transforms.

It's no longer enough to sell a molecule.

Now, you sell an ecosystem.

Where medication is one node.

Data is another.

Experience is third.

And insight—live, adaptive, human—is the bridge.

The brands that win won't just promise better outcomes.

They'll deliver experiences that feel personal, invisible, empowering.

The Quiet Revolution

In the end, the story isn't just about technology.

It's about intimacy.

A sensor that learns your rhythms.

An app that listens to your stress.

A device that nudges you toward hope.

These aren't gadgets.

They're companions.

And in a world of loneliness, burnout, and overwhelm, that companionship—the sense that someone or something cares enough to notice you in real time—might be the most powerful medicine of all.

The Stories of Abilify MyCite and Propeller Health

When the Medicine Listens Back

1. **The Pill That Knew It Had Been Swallowed: Abilify MyCite, The Schizophrenia Drug with a Secret**

   Let's begin with something ordinary.

   A pill.

   You've taken thousands in your life.

   Maybe even today—vitamins, aspirin, something for blood pressure. You swallow, forget, and trust.

   But what if the pill didn't forget?

   What if, the moment it touched your stomach, it called someone?

   Not in words. In data.

   The Story

   In 2017, the FDA approved Abilify MyCite, a treatment for schizophrenia and bipolar disorder. The active drug, aripiprazole, wasn't new. But what made headlines was what came with it: a tiny ingestible sensor embedded in the pill, and a wearable patch that sat quietly on the patient's skin.

   Here's how it worked:

   You took the pill.

   The sensor, activated by stomach fluids, sent a signal to the patch.

   The patch relayed the signal to your smartphone.

   Your smartphone told your doctor—or your caregiver—Yes, the medication was taken.

   In theory, it was elegant.

   In practice, it revealed something deeper.

   Not about the drug.

   But about trust.

   The Deeper Problem

   Schizophrenia is a condition where insight into one's own illness is often compromised. Many patients forget—or refuse—to take their meds. Non-adherence leads to relapses, hospitalizations, violence, shame.

   So the solution seemed logical:

Confirm that the medication was taken.

But here's the twist:

Many advocates and psychiatrists worried about the implications.

"Who's watching me take my pill?"

"Do I get to turn off the tracking?"

"Is this a therapeutic or a surveillance tool?"

Abilify MyCite, for all its sophistication, touched a nerve: the line between care and control.

What It Taught Us

Technology isn't neutral.

Even when it's brilliant.

It carries intention.

And it creates new relationships.

Abilify MyCite showed that convergence—pill plus patch plus app—can transform therapy. But it also revealed that data must come with dignity.

Not just: "You took your medication."

But: You're part of your healing.

You are being heard.

That's a powerful therapeutic too.

2. **The Cough That Told a Story**

   Propeller Health + GSK: Turning Asthma into a Map

   In 2014, a 38-year-old woman named Alondra was struggling with her asthma.

   She lived in Phoenix, worked in a call center, and carried her rescue inhaler in her purse. She never went anywhere without it.

   She also never quite knew when she'd need it.

   Some days were fine.

   Others—sudden wheezing, tightness, panic.

   It felt random.

   Her doctors tried different medications. Still, the pattern remained unclear.

   Until one day, she was enrolled in a pilot program through her clinic. They gave her a Propeller Health sensor.

It clipped onto her inhaler like a Fitbit for medication. It tracked every puff—when, where, how often.

And what happened next changed her story.

The Data Whisper

Alondra's usage showed a pattern no one had noticed:

- Monday mornings: high usage.
- Near the freeway: high usage.
- After nights with poor sleep: higher risk.

Her asthma wasn't random.

It was a system with triggers.

And her sensor had quietly decoded it.

The Partnership

Propeller Health had partnered with GSK and Boehringer Ingelheim to embed their sensors onto inhalers for asthma and COPD patients.

The goal?

Turn medication use into real-time epidemiology.

Patients like Alondra didn't just take their meds. They became participants in their own care.

Clinics received dashboards.

Doctors spotted worsening trends before ER visits.

Cities used anonymized data to correlate air quality with asthma attacks.

The Shift

It wasn't the inhaler that changed.

It was the feedback loop.

- Before: Patient wheezes, uses inhaler, worries alone.
- After: Patient wheezes, data gets logged, clinician sees trend, behavior changes, outcomes improve.

Propeller didn't invent a new drug.

They invented visibility.

The Bigger Lesson

Both Abilify MyCite and Propeller Health tried to solve the same mystery: What happens after the prescription?

And both did it by embedding the answer into the therapy itself.

One embedded sensors in the pill.

The other embedded intelligence into the device.

Both believed something radical:

That therapy isn't just chemical.

It's contextual.

That knowing when, where, and how someone takes their meds may be as important as what they take.

And that when medicine starts to listen—really listen—it can speak back in ways that change lives.

Epilogue: From Compliance to Collaboration

We used to think of adherence as binary:

Took the pill or didn't.

But Abilify MyCite and Propeller Health hint at a future where we ask better questions:

- Why not?
- What patterns surround the behavior?
- What does the body say that the mouth doesn't?

And that's where the magic happens.

Because once a pill can report back…

Or an inhaler can map a neighborhood…

Or a patch can sense a heartbeat of hesitation…

We no longer treat patients.

We partner with them.

Behavioral Modification and Real-Time Feedback Loops

The Mirror That Blinks Back

Let's begin with something deceptively simple.

A blinking light.

In 1965, psychologist B.F. Skinner ran a set of experiments where pigeons were placed in a box and trained to peck a button. Each time they pecked, they got a pellet of food. Peck, reward. Peck, reward. Over time, the pigeons developed patterns—some frantic, some rhythmic—depending entirely on how predictable the reward was.

Skinner called it operant conditioning.

Today, we call it behavioral design.

But swap out pigeons for people, pellets for dopamine, and the button for your smartwatch—and suddenly, Skinner's box is on your wrist.

The Feedback That Changes You

In the 1990s, a Stanford researcher named BJ Fogg coined the term "persuasive technology." His thesis? That technology could be designed not just to serve us, but to change us.

He wasn't talking about subliminal manipulation. He was talking about nudges.

A gentle vibration when you've been sitting too long.

A ring on your finger that notices poor sleep and dims your lights earlier.

An app that celebrates when you reach your 10,000 steps.

These aren't gadgets.

They're mirrors with memory.

And here's the twist: they don't just reflect your behavior.

They reshape it.

Meet the Loop

Every feedback loop has three parts:

- Trigger
- Action
- Response

You walk 2,000 steps.

Your phone buzzes.

A congratulatory ring spins on the screen.

You smile.

You walk a little more.

Tiny moment.

Big shift.

That loop might seem trivial. But stack it—hour by hour, day by day—and it becomes habit. And habit becomes identity.

"I am someone who walks."

"I am someone who sleeps eight hours."

"I am someone who manages stress."

This is behavior, not by force… but by feedback.

The Real-Time Revolution

In the old world of healthcare, feedback was slow.

You visited the doctor. They asked questions. You tried to remember.

But today?

- A patch tracks your cortisol and suggests meditation.
- A ring senses your temperature rising and prompts you to hydrate.
- A glucose monitor detects spikes and warns you of that hidden sugar in your "healthy" smoothie.

The loop now closes in seconds, not weeks.

Which means the opportunity to change is immediate.

And the behavior?

Responsive. Adaptive. Self-reinforcing.

The Magic of "Just-in-Time"

There's a term in behavioral science: Just-In-Time Adaptive Interventions (JITAIs).

These are nudges that arrive at the perfect moment—when you're most vulnerable to a lapse, or most open to a shift.

Think:

- A breath cue before a high-stakes meeting.
- A prompt to take your meds when your movement pattern suggests you forgot.
- A haptic tap when your heart rate spikes during a tense conversation.

These aren't guesses.

They're data-driven whispers.

Invisible coaching.

Silent accountability.

They don't yell.

They catch you just before the cliff.

From Behavior to Biology

And here's where it gets fascinating.

These micro-behaviors—sleep, breath, steps, mood—aren't just outcomes.

They're inputs that change biology.

- Better sleep alters gene expression.
- Regular movement reduces inflammation.
- Calmer breath recalibrates heart rate variability.

So the loop doesn't end at behavior.

It loops right back to cellular health.

This is where behavioral science meets molecular science.

Where the Fitbit becomes as powerful as the pharmacy.

The True Transformation

Remember the tipping points, the moment when a trend becomes a movement.

Here, the tipping point is invisible.

It's not a dramatic act.

It's the compounding of quiet feedback.

Day after day, moment after moment.

Until one day you wake up and realize:

You are no longer the person who needed reminding.

You've become the person who does the thing.

That's the power of the loop.

It doesn't push.

It invites.

And in that invitation, behavior becomes belief.

The Pharma Implication

For pharma, this changes everything.

You're not just selling molecules anymore.

You're designing loops of care.

- Drug + wearable.
- App + behavior.
- Data + story.

You're not saying: "Take this."

You're asking: "What's happening now? How can we help, right this second?"

And in that moment—right now, not later—you gain something rare:

Agency. Attention. Adherence. Trust.

Epilogue: The Echo

The blinking light.

The vibration on your wrist.

The small ring on your finger that knows you better than your diary.

It's not about the tech.

It's about the echo.

The behavior you perform.

The response you receive.

The meaning you construct.

And when that echo is right…

You don't just change your habit.

You change your story.

Chapter 6

The Compliance Conundrum – Solved

It began with a plastic cup.

In a quiet hospital room in Detroit in the early 1980s, a nurse stood at the edge of a bed, holding a cup with three pills and a glass of water. The patient—a soft-spoken man in his 60s recovering from a mild stroke—nodded, took the cup, and swallowed the pills.

Or so it seemed.

Fifteen minutes later, while changing the linens, the nurse found two soggy tablets tucked under the pillow. Not chewed. Not dissolved. Hidden.

This was the quiet epidemic.

Not disease.

Non-compliance.

The Invisible Epidemic

For decades, pharmaceutical companies had solved for chemistry. They built better molecules. More targeted. More powerful. More precise.

But the pills didn't work if they weren't taken.

And they often weren't.

The World Health Organization estimates that 50% of people with chronic conditions don't take their medications as prescribed.

Fifty percent.

Not due to cost. Not due to side effects.

But due to forgetfulness, skepticism, confusion, mistrust, shame.

Doctors wrote prescriptions.

Patients quietly edited them.

And so, pharma's greatest challenge wasn't chemical.

It was behavioral.

The Myth of the "Bad Patient"

In the traditional model, we labeled these people as non-compliant.

We shook our heads. We wrote reminder notes. We designed plastic pillboxes with compartments for each day.

But that's the wrong story.

What if the issue wasn't disobedience?

What if it was disconnect?

What if the pill, once outside the pharmacy, entered a vast void?

A void of feedback, motivation, relevance, context.

What if… the medicine simply became invisible?

The Loop that Changed Everything

In 2017, something subtle happened.

A new phrase emerged: digital medication adherence systems.

Not very catchy. But revolutionary in practice.

The first FDA-approved drug with a sensor—Abilify MyCite—could track ingestion. But more importantly, it started a domino effect.

Suddenly, the act of taking a pill could be seen.

And once seen, it could be responded to.

And once responded to… it could be reinforced.

We weren't tracking for surveillance.

We were building a loop of accountability and care.

It was no longer about punishing the forgetful.

It was about empowering the overwhelmed.

From Push to Pull

A decade ago, pharma companies pushed compliance:

Brochures, reminder texts, refill calls.

Today, wearables pull behavior by meeting patients where they are—on the wrist, on the skin, on the phone.

- A smartwatch vibrates when the usual time to take meds passes without confirmation.
- A patch detects vital signs and adjusts prompts based on stress levels.

An AI companion app notices skipped doses and offers a human-like check-in:

"Rough day? Want to reschedule your dose for an hour later?"

The tone shifted—from discipline to dialogue.

The Psychology of Being Seen

Here's the insight:

When people feel watched, they behave differently.

But when people feel seen, they behave authentically.

That distinction matters.

A blinking sensor isn't enough.

But a wearable that notices, adapts, and responds with warmth and intelligence?

That's not a device. That's a partner.

Real-Time Redemption

In the old paradigm, a missed dose was a mark of failure.

Now, it's a signal.

A starting point.

A conversation.

Missed your statin dose?

The app asks: "Want to reschedule for later today or tomorrow morning?"

That tiny moment of redemption—where failure becomes flexibility—may be the most powerful pharmaceutical innovation in years.

Case Study: The Loop in Action

Consider a pilot study at a large U.S. health system.

They deployed smart pill bottles with Bluetooth sensors to patients with heart failure. Each missed dose triggered a notification to a nurse dashboard, which, in turn, prompted a short check-in call.

Compliance jumped from 54% to 87% in 3 months.

Not because the pills changed.

But because the relationship did.

Patients weren't alone in their behavior.

They were in the loop.

Compliance Reimagined

The solution to non-compliance, it turns out, isn't to try harder to make patients obey.

It's to redesign the environment so that adherence becomes the natural, even joyful, thing to do.

- Make feedback instant.
- Make engagement empathetic.
- Make the consequences visible—not as threats, but as motivation.

Epilogue: A New Language

We used to call it "compliance."

Then we softened it to "adherence."

Now, we're moving toward something even better:

Participation.

Because when a wearable nudges gently,

When a patch responds intelligently,

When a drug listens and adapts—

We're not enforcing behavior.

We're inviting it.

And when the invitation is thoughtful, kind, and timely?

People say yes.

And swallow the pill.

Not because they must.

But because they choose to.

Medication Adherence, Behavioral Nudges, and Predictive Alerts

The Gentle Art of Being Reminded

The Problem Isn't the Pill. It's the Pause.

Imagine this.

You've just left your doctor's office, prescription in hand. The instructions are clear. Take one tablet in the morning, one in the evening. For the next 90 days. Simple.

But sometime around Day 17, life happens.

A long meeting. A stressful phone call. A missed refill.

And just like that, the routine unravels.

Not because you're defiant.

Not because you're lazy.

But because you're human.

This is the story of non-adherence—one of the most costly, misunderstood, and fixable problems in healthcare.

A 300-Billion-Dollar Silence

Let's start with a number: $300 billion.

That's the estimated annual cost of medication non-adherence in the U.S. alone—from avoidable hospitalizations, complications, and readmissions.

And it's not about ignorance.

Most patients want to take their meds. They know they should.

But knowledge isn't behavior.

Intention isn't execution.

And this is where the revolution begins—not with better drugs, but with better reminders.

The Power of the Nudge

In 2008, Richard Thaler and Cass Sunstein published a book called Nudge. Their central thesis was deceptively simple: people make better decisions not when they're forced… but when they're nudged.

Not commanded.

Not coerced.

Nudged.

Think of the GPS in your car:

It doesn't force you to take the next turn.

It suggests.

And it reroutes—without scolding—when you miss it.

Now imagine a wearable that functions like that.

- A gentle vibration on your wrist when your 8 a.m. dose is due.
- A soft chime that links to your movement pattern—knowing you're in your kitchen.
- A message: "Looks like you're preparing breakfast. Don't forget your thyroid pill."

That's not just a reminder.

That's contextual persuasion.

That's a nudge.

The Psychology of the Timely Tap

Behavioral science tells us that timing is everything.

Remind someone too early, and they'll ignore it.

Too late, and the moment is lost.

Wearables, powered by data and AI, solve this.

They know when you usually take your meds.

They detect when your routine breaks.

And then they gently intervene.

Not with judgment. But with presence.

Just like a friend who shows up—not with a lecture—but with a hand on your shoulder.

Predictive Alerts: When the System Knows Before You Do

Here's where things get uncanny.

Let's say your smart inhaler has noticed you've needed more puffs this week.

Your resting heart rate has risen slightly.

Your sleep score is down.

Separately, these are noise.

Together? They spell early asthma exacerbation.

Before you even feel it.

Before you even miss a dose.

The system alerts your doctor.

Adjusts your dose.

Sends a nudge.

"We've noticed changes that might increase your risk. Let's adjust your plan today."

That's no longer reactive healthcare.

That's predictive compassion.

Case Study: When the Pill Talks Back

In Japan, researchers piloted a program using digital pillboxes synced with wearables and caregiver dashboards for elderly hypertensive patients.

Each missed dose triggered:

- A color change on the pillbox (subtle cue).
- A voice reminder on the patient's TV (contextual nudge).
- A text to a family member after two consecutive misses.

Adherence went from 62% to 91% in 6 weeks.

Not by guilt.

Not by fear.

But by gentle, layered nudges.

The Soft Revolution in Pharma

For decades, the pharmaceutical industry chased better efficacy.

Now, it's chasing better engagement.

Because a 90% effective drug, when taken only 60% of the time, delivers… 54% efficacy.

But add a wearable.

Add a nudge.

Add an alert that learns you…

And suddenly, that 54% becomes personalized precision.

The Twist

In The Tipping Point, Malcolm Gladwell argued that the little things can make a big difference.

Here, the little things are:

- A vibration.
- A flash of light.
- A kind message.
- A pattern noticed before a problem.

And the big difference is:

- Fewer heart attacks.
- Fewer ER visits.
- Fewer forgotten doses.
- And millions of people silently supported by technology that understands.

Not just tools.

Not just pills.

But an ecosystem of nudges that whispers at the right moment, until change becomes habit—and habit becomes health.

Real-World Data on Adherence and Wearables — How Adherence Rose by 18% in Trials Using Wearable Reminders

When the Body Listens Back: A Button that Changed Nothing

In 2012, a large hospital chain in the Midwest launched what they believed was a breakthrough in medication adherence: a big red button.

It was installed at the exit of their outpatient pharmacy.

On it, in bold letters: "REMEMBER TO TAKE YOUR MEDICATION."

Patients chuckled. Some pressed it. A few took selfies.

The idea was simple: visibility breeds memory.

But within six months, there was no measurable improvement.

The button had failed.

Why?

Because the reminder wasn't the problem.

The context was.

The Ghost in the Routine

Behavioral scientists have long known that memory isn't linear.

We don't forget everything at once. We forget in the cracks—those micro-moments where habit collapses into chaos.

- A child cries in the middle of the pill schedule.
- The commute runs late.
- The weekend disrupts the rhythm.

The issue isn't disobedience.

It's disruption.

And then—quietly, invisibly—compliance slides.

One dose skipped becomes two.

Two becomes a week.

And soon, a chronic condition festers in the silence of forgetfulness.

The 18% Breakthrough

In 2018, a multinational clinical trial—run across five countries and involving over 4,200 patients with hypertension—introduced something different.

Not a lecture. Not a leaflet.

But a wearable.

Specifically, a discreet smart wristband that:

- Detected movement.
- Synced with medication timing.
- Nudged patients with gentle haptic pulses at personalized intervals.
- Adapted based on daily routine, missed doses, and even mood (via passive data).

The results?

An 18% increase in adherence over six months.

No new drug. No additional cost. No change in formulation.

Just a better relationship between time, habit, and attention.

Why 18% Matters more than You Think

To a casual observer, 18% may sound modest.

But to a cardiologist treating a hypertensive patient whose adherence hovered around 60%, that 18% means:

- Fewer strokes.
- Fewer emergency visits.
- Fewer nights in the ICU.
- And thousands saved in treatment costs.

It's the difference between eventually and never again.

The Moment the Reminder becomes Real

One participant, a 67-year-old retired bus driver in Barcelona, reported:

"At first, I ignored the buzz. But one day, I felt it while pouring my coffee, and it felt like a tap on the shoulder from someone who cared."

That's not just feedback.

That's empathy in vibration form.

Because what wearables offer isn't just data.

It's intelligent companionship.

From Big Data to Small Nudges

Here's the counterintuitive insight:

The more complex the backend system—AI, behavior modeling, predictive analytics—the more simple the front-end experience must be.

- A blink of light.
- A gentle buzz.
- A notification that waits, not nags.

The success of the 18% wasn't in the technology.

It was in the humanization of that technology.

It wasn't about tracking behavior.

It was about joining it.

The Pattern that Emerged

Researchers noticed something fascinating:

- The first skipped dose rarely responded to reminders.
- But if a predictive alert fired before the second miss, re-engagement shot up by 42%.

In other words:

We don't just need reminders.

We need timely interventions before drift becomes a pattern.

The wearable didn't wait until people failed.

It intervened in the hesitation.

And that is the magic moment—the pause between intention and forgetfulness—where transformation lives.

What this Means for Pharma?

For years, pharmaceutical innovation meant better molecules.

Now, it also means better motivation.

Not in the form of incentives.

But in the form of micro-encouragement.

The wristband doesn't cure hypertension.

But it may be the most effective therapeutic amplifier pharma has discovered in a decade.

Why?

Because it speaks in the language patients understand best:

Now. Here. You. This.

A New Chapter in Human-Centered Care

The red button didn't work because it reminded everyone… at once.

The wearable works because it reminds you, in your moment, in your language, in your rhythm.

And that may be the real breakthrough.

Not the pill.

Not the patch.

Not the wearable.

But the realization that the smallest buzz, at the right second, can do what megadoses of information never could:

Help people help themselves—before they even realize they're about to fall.

Case Study: The AiCure Story — When the Camera became the Caregiver

The Face that Took the Pill

The Problem of the Unseen Swallow

Let's start in a hospital corridor in New York City.

It's 2011.

A young researcher named Adam Hanina is pacing.

He's frustrated—but curious.

He's spent the last two years helping pharmaceutical firms solve a very old, very expensive problem:

"We give patients pills. We ask if they've taken them. They say yes. But did they… really?"

In clinical trials, adherence isn't just a good-to-have.

It's everything.

If patients don't take the drug as prescribed, the data becomes meaningless.

Dosage appears ineffective. Side effects are misreported.

Promising drugs fail not because they don't work—but because they weren't taken.

So Adam asks the million-dollar question:

"What if we didn't need to ask them at all?"

What if we could just see?

The Birth of AiCure: A Mirror with a Brain

Enter: AiCure—a startup with a peculiar but brilliant idea.

Use the front-facing camera on a smartphone.

Train it with AI and facial recognition.

Add computer vision, behavioral analytics, and machine learning.

And teach it to know—really know—when a person puts a pill in their mouth… and swallows.

No fancy hardware.

No biometric bands.

Just the humble camera, watching the face.

Not spying.

Not judging.

Just verifying—with clinical accuracy.

The Twist: Trust Without Asking

We live in a world that's built on trust.

We trust patients. We trust memory. We trust checkboxes.

But trust—especially in clinical research—is fragile.

Patients forget.

Nurses get overworked.

Doctors rely on self-reporting.

What AiCure did was introduce a third party.

Not a person.

Not a form.

But a mirror that remembers.

You look at your phone.

It recognizes your face.

You show the pill.

You place it on your tongue.

You swallow.

And the app—silently, precisely—confirms ingestion.

That moment is logged.

Time-stamped.

Encrypted.

And sent back to the trial coordinator in real time.

No diary needed.

No reminder calls.

Just frictionless fidelity.

The Unexpected Hero: Facial AI

Now pause for a second and consider:

This isn't a deep-learning algorithm detecting cancer cells.

This is a machine watching for something as simple—and profound—as a human swallow.

And that's the genius of it.

What AiCure recognized is that behavioral adherence is visible.

It lives in the mundane.

The blink.

The tilt of the head.

The motion of a hand.

The seal of lips.

The pause.

The gulp.

In those micro-movements, truth lives.

And now, so does verification.

The Data Speaks

In one NIH-funded trial involving schizophrenia patients—a population known for non-adherence rates above 50%—AiCure was deployed to track oral antipsychotic use.

The result?

- Adherence rose to over 89%.
- Hospitalizations dropped.
- Trial integrity soared.
- And for the first time, pharma had a verifiable behavioral biomarker.

Not based on theory.

Not based on interviews.

But based on faces.

The Human Moment in a Digital Mirror

Now here's the part that no one predicted.

Many patients—especially elderly ones—didn't find the AI invasive.

They found it… comforting.

"I feel like someone's watching out for me," one woman in the trial said.

"It's not just a phone. It's… there."

Because AiCure didn't just monitor.

It acknowledged.

It said: "We see you."

"We know you're trying."

"You are not alone in this."

That's not surveillance.

That's presence.

The Implications for Pharma

With AiCure, the clinical trial paradigm shifted.

Drugs no longer had to trust memory.

They could now rely on measured behavior.

This means:

- Faster approvals.
- Cleaner data.
- Fewer patients needed to reach statistical power.
- And most of all, real-world adherence that reflects real-world use.

The Tipping Point of Trust

In The Tipping Point, Malcolm Gladwell explored how small things—like a broken window or a pair of hush puppies—could tip behavior.

AiCure is one such tipping point.

A camera.

A face.

A blink.

A swallow.

And suddenly, the invisible becomes visible.

The assumed becomes proven.

The question—"Did they take it?"—becomes undeniably answered.

Not with suspicion.

But with subtle certainty.

Epilogue: The Machine that Watched Over Me

Years after that first pilot, AiCure had expanded into multiple therapeutic areas—HIV, cardiovascular disease, hepatitis C, even opioid use disorder.

Everywhere it went, the story repeated:

When technology respects behavior,

When it fits into life—without judging, without interrupting—

It becomes not a monitor, but a partner.

That's not just innovation.

That's empathy coded into pixels.

And that… is the future of adherence.

PART III: REAL-WORLD CASE STUDIES

Part III

Real-world Case Studies

When Data Becomes Destiny

In the summer of 1983, a pediatrician in rural Finland began to notice something strange.

Her young patients—normally energetic, wriggly, sugar-hunting children—had begun returning to her clinic wearing small black straps on their chests.

No, it wasn't a medical order.

It was a gift from their parents, who had taken up jogging.

These were the earliest Polar heart rate monitors, and the children unknowingly became part of the world's first passive health data experiment.

No one thought of it that way. Not yet.

Back then, it was a quirky Finnish trend.

But that's the funny thing about data.

It begins as noise.

A beat. A breath. A buzz.

A graph that wiggles. A number that fluctuates.

Then, someone notices a pattern.

A correlation. A drift. A slope.

And suddenly, it's not noise anymore.

It's a story.

The Story Hidden in Sweat, Steps, and Skin

In the world of wearable technology, we often celebrate the engineering—flexible batteries, nanotech sensors, motion-sensing gyroscopes.

But the real breakthrough isn't in the gadget.

It's in what the gadget reveals—not just about the body, but about human behavior, clinical reality, and market strategy.

This is where Part III begins.

Because what follows isn't speculation.

It's not potential.

It's not theory.

It's the moment when data moves from abstraction to consequence.

The Quiet Revolution in Pharma

Consider this:

A patient with asthma begins to skip her inhaler—not due to negligence, but because of a subconscious belief that symptoms = medication, not the other way around.

- A wearable detects the lapse.
- A gentle nudge is sent.
- Medication resumes.
- No ER visit.
- No hospitalization.

That's not just health optimization.

That's destiny rewritten.

And it happens not in the lab, but in the wild—in homes, workplaces, classrooms, airports, night shifts, and Sunday parks.

The "Small Data" That Mattered Most

What these case studies will show is this:

It wasn't the sheer volume of data that made the difference.

It was the timing. The context. The insight.

One patient's nightly heart-rate variability prompted an early heart failure alert.

One behavioral flag predicted a depressive relapse.

One subtle change in skin conductivity revealed rising anxiety before the patient even had the language for it.

The future wasn't forecasted.

It was felt, first and only later understood.

The Law of the Hidden Variable

I've long been fascinated by Gladwell's Law of the Hidden Variable:

That the thing we don't measure is often the thing that matters most.

But what happens when sensors catch the invisible?

What happens when the variable isn't hidden anymore?

That's what these stories explore:

- A pill that sends a signal after it's swallowed.
- A bracelet that predicts seizures before they begin.
- A patch that knows your heartbeat better than you do.

And a pharmaceutical industry that no longer sells only molecules,

but monitoring, motivation, and meaning.

From Case Study to Case Destiny

These stories aren't success stories in the traditional sense.

They're pivot points—moments when a technology intersected with human vulnerability and something changed.

You'll meet:

- The COPD patient who avoided a third hospitalization.
- The schizophrenia trial that didn't fail—because this time, the meds were actually taken.
- The pharma brand manager who realized the product wasn't the drug—but the experience of the drug in a real body, in real time.

Each chapter in this section begins with a case.

Each ends with a question:

"What does it mean when your body becomes your best source of truth?"

Welcome to the World Where Data Thinks First

This is medicine with memory.

Marketing with metrics.

Science with skin in the game.

It's not the future anymore.

It's the present—measured in microns, milliseconds, and molecules.

And as these cases reveal, when data becomes destiny,

the most profound changes don't happen in the lab.

They happen in us.

Chapter 7

Roche's Smartwatch Trials in Parkinson's

The Watch that Listened to Silence

Roche, Parkinson's, and the Science of Movement That Stopped Moving

In 2018, a man named Andreas sat at his kitchen table in Basel, Switzerland, sipping his morning coffee.

He wasn't a doctor.

He wasn't a patient.

He wasn't an engineer.

He was a listener—or at least, that's what his colleagues at Roche began calling him.

Because Andreas had become obsessed with something no one else could hear:

The sound of a tremor not yet visible,

The whisper of slowness in a gait,

The near-silent pause in a finger tap.

Andreas didn't use a stethoscope.

He used a watch.

More specifically, he used a smartwatch—strapped not to a wrist, but to a new vision of pharmaceutical care.

The Parkinson's Puzzle

Here's the thing about Parkinson's disease: it hides.

It doesn't arrive as a headline.

It creeps in, slowly, subtly—

One dropped key.

One stumble on the stairs.

One morning where the hand refuses to play along.

And here's the problem for pharma:

By the time the symptoms are clinically measurable, the damage is already significant.

The brain has been losing dopamine-producing neurons for years.

But no one noticed. Not even the patient.

Roche's question, then, was deceptively simple:

"Can we measure the unmeasurable? Can a watch know what a neurologist can't see?"

The Smartwatch Becomes a Microscope

Let's rewind.

In 2017, Roche partnered with Genentech and digital health firm MC10, setting out on what would become one of the largest digital biomarker trials for Parkinson's in history.

Participants wore specially configured smartwatches—ones that didn't care about your steps or calories.

They cared about:

- How regularly you walked.
- How precisely your fingers tapped a screen.
- How your voice trembled when reading a passage aloud.
- How your stillness shifted during sleep.

This wasn't fitness tracking.

This was neurology on the wrist.

The Inversion: Movement as Diagnosis

We usually think of diagnosis as something that happens in the clinic.

With machines, scans, doctors.

But Roche flipped that assumption.

They asked:

"What if the most honest place to understand Parkinson's... is in the kitchen?"

"What if a smartwatch worn at home, during life—not illness—tells the truth?"

Suddenly, movement became data.

And data became diagnosis—or at least, a new language for it.

What the Watch Discovered?

Here's where it gets fascinating.

As Roche's clinical trials expanded, they began to see patterns:

- Micro-slowness in finger tapping predicted worsening symptoms weeks in advance.
- Subtle changes in voice tone correlated with bradykinesia progression.
- Changes in movement during sleep indicated emotional and motor deterioration.

The smartwatch wasn't just recording motion.

It was listening to deterioration.

It was forecasting disease.

Think about that:

A wristwatch, forecasting neurodegeneration like a weather app predicts rain.

The Human Side of the Loop

One participant—let's call him Luis—said something unforgettable in an interview:

"I feel like the watch knows me better than my neurologist."

Not because his doctor wasn't brilliant.

But because the watch was always there.

At breakfast. At bedtime.

On good days. On bad ones.

In between clinic visits—where the truth often hides.

It was continuous. Honest. Unfiltered.

And for patients with a disease that plays tricks on the body and the mind, that continuity was everything.

The Tipping Point: When Pharma Became a Sensor Company

This chapter in Roche's journey marked more than a clinical trial.

It was a pivot point.

The company wasn't just testing a drug.

It was testing a new paradigm—where digital biomarkers could complement or even surpass traditional ones.

Where a patient's everyday life could produce more useful data than a $10,000 hospital scan.

Where pharma wasn't just developing molecules, but systems of sensing.

Why this Matters?

Imagine this becoming the norm:

- Wearables detect disease progression days or weeks in advance.
- Clinical trials become faster, cheaper, more precise, with less patient burden.
- Regulators begin accepting digital endpoints as valid measures of efficacy.

Roche didn't just validate a technology.

They validated a future, where the body speaks through devices, and silence is no longer invisible.

Epilogue: A New Listening Device

In The Tipping Point, Gladwell about the power of context—that the invisible forces around us shape human behavior.

What Roche discovered is that Parkinson's, too, is a disease of context.

It's not just about what happens in a hospital.

It's about what happens at home.

In the tremor no one saw.

In the slowness, no one noticed.

Unless, of course, a watch was listening.

Roche's Collaboration with Apple on Tracking Tremors and Gait Changes in Parkinson's Patients

The Silent Symphony: How Roche and Apple Measured What Neurologists Missed

In a brightly lit apartment in San Jose, a man named Ray stood perfectly still.

Not because he wanted to.

But because he couldn't move.

Moments earlier, Ray had been walking across his kitchen to refill his coffee. And then, just like that, his feet forgot how to walk. His brain sent the signal—but somewhere along the neural pathway, the instruction lost its way.

It lasted for 12 seconds.

And here's the strange part: Ray didn't report it.

Not to his doctor. Not even to his wife.

But his watch did.

The Odd Couple: Big Pharma Meets Big Tech

It was easy to miss the announcement.

A pharmaceutical giant (Roche) teaming up with Apple, a consumer electronics titan, to monitor Parkinson's disease progression through iPhones and Apple Watches.

To most, it sounded like a PR stunt.

But those who understood both the disease and the device saw something else entirely.

They saw a diagnostic revolution wrapped around your wrist.

The Unseen Burden of Parkinson's

Let's pause here.

Parkinson's isn't just tremors and stiffness.

It's also unpredictability.

A kind of neurological betrayal-by-surprise.

A patient may move easily for an hour… and then freeze mid-step.

Clinicians call it freezing of gait (FoG)—but patients don't always report it.

Why?

Because it's hard to describe something that appears, vanishes, and isn't there when you're in the doctor's office.

This is the paradox that plagued neurologists and pharmaceutical researchers for decades:

How do you treat what you can't see?

Enter the Watch that Sees Everything

In 2021, Roche and Apple began integrating Apple's Movement Disorder API—a feature built into the Apple Watch designed to passively and continuously collect motor data like:

- Tremor amplitude
- Tremor frequency
- Gait asymmetry
- Walking speed
- Double support time (how long both feet touch the ground during a step)

Now imagine this:

A patient with Parkinson's wears the Apple Watch every day—not just during clinic visits.

The watch doesn't beep or buzz.

It doesn't interrupt.

It watches.

Waits.

Listens.

It becomes a silent companion, logging every step, stumble, tremble, and stillness.

The Hidden Tipping Point

In Blink, Gladwell explored how snap judgments—those fast, unconscious impressions—can often be more accurate than hours of deliberation.

With Parkinson's, the reverse is true.

You need long, quiet watching—not snap assessments.

That's what Apple's algorithms, trained on terabytes of health data, began to offer.

And that's what Roche needed for their digital clinical endpoints—real-world, real-time, passive data, collected with zero burden on patients.

This changed everything.

Instead of asking patients, "How was your week?"

Now the data told them.

Clinical Trials Without the Clinic

This partnership wasn't just about helping patients.

It was about reinventing how clinical trials were run.

Traditionally, Parkinson's trials rely on the MDS-UPDRS scale—a subjective scoring system done during clinic visits, full of "on the day" observations and human interpretation.

But Roche's digital endpoints using Apple Watch data offered something radical:

- Objective measurements
- Continuous tracking
- Real-life context—not lab-coat context

In one study, Roche researchers could detect gait changes 7–10 days earlier than clinicians could through scheduled visits.

Think about that:

A consumer watch caught a disease before a specialist did.

That's not just impressive.

That's disruptive.

The Inversion of Expertise

For centuries, medicine placed authority in the hands of specialists.

But with wearables, the body becomes its own expert.

Roche didn't just digitize Parkinson's monitoring.

They decentralized it.

Suddenly:

- The clinic became the living room
- The lab became the sidewalk
- The scan became the stride
- The sensor became the storyteller

It wasn't just about seeing more.

It was about seeing differently.

Ray's Second Freeze

Let's return to Ray.

A week after that first freezing episode, it happened again.

This time, his neurologist already knew.

Because the data had already told the story:

- Gait rhythm disrupted
- Tremor increasing in his left wrist
- Increased asymmetry
- Longer double support time

Roche's dashboard flagged it.

An intervention was adjusted.

Medication titrated.

Crisis avoided.

Ray didn't have to remember anything.

Because his watch did.

The Final Layer: When Pharma Feels Personal

We often think of pharma as distant—corporate, analytical, molecule-driven.

But Roche's collaboration with Apple rehumanized it.

By listening to the steps between the scans,

By watching the silences between the symptoms,

They brought medicine home.

And in doing so, they didn't just improve Parkinson's care.

They redefined what it means to measure movement…

… in a disease where movement slowly disappears.

How Data Redefined Recruitment, Endpoints, and Engagement

The Invisible Revolution: How Wearable Data Quietly Rewired the Engine of Clinical Trials

There's a paradox at the heart of every pharmaceutical breakthrough.

Before a drug changes lives, it must first enter the most controlled, scrutinized, and artificial environment imaginable:

The clinical trial.

Here, rules reign.

Checklists dominate.

Inclusion criteria stretch for pages.

Endpoints are rigid.

And patients become… data points.

For decades, this was considered the price of precision. But somewhere along the way, researchers noticed something curious:

The world inside the trial didn't always match the world outside it.

That's when wearables entered the story—not as flashy gadgets, but as silent reformers.

Recruitment: The Art of Finding the Right Stranger

Let's begin with recruitment.

In 2016, a CRO (Contract Research Organization) tasked with recruiting for a rare autoimmune trial in the U.S. found itself staring at a wall.

The inclusion criteria were strict:

- Disease stage: early-to-mid progression
- Biomarkers: specific thresholds
- Activity levels: moderately functional

The trouble?

These filters filtered out everyone.

Then someone had an idea:

What if, instead of waiting for patients to walk in… we listened to their wearables?

Partnering with a health data platform, they identified individuals—across wearable ecosystems like Fitbit, Apple Health, and Garmin—whose activity patterns matched the early stages of decline. Subtle fatigue. Decreased step consistency. Erratic sleep.

They weren't patients yet.

They were pre-patients—and they were perfect for early-intervention trials.

Recruitment rates tripled.

Time-to-fill dropped by 60%.

Dropouts? Minimal.

That's not just efficiency. That's a tipping point.

Endpoints: From Snapshots to Symphonies

Now to the second act: endpoints.

Traditionally, trials rely on what we might call "snapshot metrics"—blood tests, symptom scores, imaging—captured at fixed moments.

It's like evaluating a symphony by listening to three random seconds of sound.

But wearables changed the music.

Now, endpoints could be:

- Sleep quality over 60 nights
- Gait symmetry during daily walks
- Tremor amplitude during mealtimes
- Heart rate variability before and after medication

This wasn't a snapshot. It was a full recording.

One trial in oncology used wearable skin sensors to monitor fatigue in chemo patients—measured not by self-report, but by movement trends, heart rate dips, and passivity scores over weeks.

And the surprise?

These passive metrics predicted treatment toxicity days before symptoms appeared.

Suddenly, endpoints weren't just measures of what had happened—they became indicators of what was about to happen.

That's not just data. That's foresight.

Engagement: The Trial that Followed You Home

Then came engagement—the silent killer of many a good study.

Patients forget appointments.

They drop out.

They move.

They lose interest.

They simply stop showing up.

Because, for decades, trials asked patients to come to the data.

Wearables flipped the model:

Now the data came to the patient.

A diabetes study in Europe gave participants continuous glucose monitors and smartwatches. No diaries. No reminders.

But they did something unexpected: they let patients see the data in real time.

One participant described it this way:

"Before, I was a subject in someone else's study. Now, I feel like I'm the scientist of my own body."

Compliance soared.

Engagement improved by 40%.

Dropouts fell by 70%.

People stayed in trials not because they were told to…

…but because they became part of the story.

The Inversion: When Control Becomes Context

In The Tipping Point, Gladwell wrote that little things can make a big difference.

In the world of pharma trials, data granularity—once considered a nuisance—has become a superpower.

- Recruitment no longer begins with a blood test, but a step count.
- Endpoints no longer wait for Day 90—they whisper every hour.
- Engagement isn't a form letter. It's a mirror held up to the body.

This is the silent, invisible revolution in pharma R&D.

It's not flashy.

It's not loud.

But it's rewiring the architecture of evidence itself.

And all of it began when someone decided to stop treating data as a clipboard—and started treating it as a conversation.

Chapter 8

Dexcom, Diabetes, and the Real-Time Revolution

Where a Drop of Blood Meets the Speed of Thought

The moment that changed Jackson's life was unremarkable at first glance.

He was standing in line at a movie theater with his 11-year-old daughter, Lucy. She tugged at his sleeve, not because she wanted popcorn, but because his Apple Watch vibrated.

The message was short: Glucose: 63 mg/dL. Falling.

They hadn't even bought their tickets yet.

Jackson excused himself, reached for a juice box he kept in his coat pocket, and downed it quietly. He returned to the line just in time for the previews.

To Lucy, it was nothing.

To Jackson, it was a miracle of anticipation.

Before Dexcom, There was Blood

To understand why that moment mattered, you need to rewind a few decades—to the world before continuous glucose monitors (CGMs).

Back then, diabetes management was like playing darts in the dark.

You pricked your finger four times a day, maybe five.

Each test gave you a number—a snapshot, frozen in time.

But blood sugar is not a photograph. It's a movie.

You don't just want to know where it is.

You want to know where it's going.

The Birth of a Sensor

Dexcom didn't invent CGM.

But they made it human.

In 2006, they launched their first system—a sensor worn under the skin that continuously measured interstitial glucose levels and sent that data to a handheld receiver.

It was revolutionary. But flawed.

Readings were delayed.

Alarms were clunky.

Patients still needed fingersticks to confirm the numbers.

But then, something happened. Not all at once.

A string of small, almost invisible shifts—each one a tiny tipping point.

- Better sensors: Smaller, more accurate, longer-lasting.
- Mobile integration: iPhones became receivers.
- Cloud sharing: Parents of diabetic kids could see glucose trends in real time—even when their child was at school.
- Open APIs: Platforms like Tidepool and Apple Health enabled visualizations, predictions, and nudges.

By 2020, Dexcom's G6 system could:

- Deliver real-time glucose readings every 5 minutes.
- Send alerts before blood sugar dropped.
- Integrate seamlessly into smartwatches, insulin pumps, and data dashboards.
- Enable remote monitoring, turning diabetes from a solitary condition into a connected experience.

The Real-Time Revolution Begins

Remember: ideas spread like viruses—quietly, socially, exponentially.

That's exactly how Dexcom changed diabetes care.

Not with a bang, but with a stream of data.

Suddenly, endocrinologists could see how meals affected glucose curves—not just guesses in a food diary.

Parents could be woken up before a hypoglycemic crash at 3 AM.

And perhaps most powerfully, patients could see themselves differently.

Data was no longer a punishment.

It was feedback.

Compassion.

Control.

The Empowered Patient

Dexcom didn't just change the device.

It changed the dialogue.

In the past, doctors lectured.

Now, they listened.

- Why did your glucose spike after lunch?
- Oh, it was stress from a meeting? That's in the data.
- What if we tried meditation at 1 PM instead of adjusting insulin?

The data didn't scold. It explained.

And in that explanation, a new kind of behavior change emerged: not compliance, but collaboration.

This is behavioral psychology in motion—what Gladwell would call a "sticky" intervention.

It sticks because it's personal.

Timely.

Visual.

Unavoidable—but not judgmental.

From Management to Prediction

Here's the part that feels like science fiction.

Dexcom's real-time data, when fed into machine learning models, can now predict hypoglycemia up to 30 minutes in advance.

That's not just management.

That's foresight.

Now imagine layering this with:

- Behavioral nudges ("You're trending low. Grab a snack.")
- Automated insulin adjustments (with closed-loop systems like Tandem's Control-IQ)
- Population-level insights for pharma trials and public health campaigns

This is no longer about treating diabetes.

It's about preventing its worst outcomes before they happen.

What Dexcom Really Did?

What's the real story beneath the obvious one?

So here's the obvious story: Dexcom made a better diabetes device.

But the real story is this:

Dexcom helped us rethink what healthcare could be when it stops reacting… and starts anticipating.

They turned a blood sugar number into a conversation.

They turned time into a tool.

And they turned patients into protagonists—navigating their condition not by fear, but by informed choice.

Lucy's Dad, Revisited

Jackson still wears his Dexcom every day.

Lucy is 17 now. She's applying to college.

At her entrance interview, when asked about her personal essay—titled "The Night My Dad Didn't Faint in the Movie Theater"—she smiles.

Because that essay wasn't about diabetes.

It was about what happens when technology gets close enough to care.

From Finger-Pricks to Continuous Glucose Monitoring (CGM)

From Finger-Pricks to Forecasts

The Slow, Silent Revolution of Knowing What Comes Next

Let's start with a sound.

A sharp click of a lancet.

A muted ouch.

A red bead of blood.

A pause.

A number.

A sigh.

For millions of people with diabetes, this was the rhythm of their day.

Four, five, sometimes ten times. Every single day.

The finger-prick wasn't just a method—it was a way of life.

And like all rituals, it was both familiar and flawed.

Because what if that number—98, or 175, or 48—was wrong?

Not wrong in the sense of a faulty reading. But wrong in what it meant.

You see, finger-pricks told you where you were, but never where you were going.

The Snapshot Problem

To understand the revolution that CGM brought, you have to understand what came before.

The finger-prick test was like checking the weather by looking out the window.

Yes, it told you it was raining.

But not when the storm started.

Not how long it would last.

And definitely not when it might flood.

So patients became guessers, not decision-makers.

They didn't know whether they were trending up or down.

Whether that apple at lunch would send them into a spike.

Or whether they might crash while asleep.

Diabetes was a mystery novel—but only one page was visible at a time.

The Birth of a New Storyline

The first continuous glucose monitors (CGMs) arrived in the early 2000s.

They weren't perfect.

They were bulky.

They lagged behind actual blood sugar.

You still had to calibrate with finger-pricks.

And worst of all, you couldn't see the data live.

But they hinted at something radical:

A world in which diabetes didn't surprise you.

A world in which data could whisper before it shouted.

That was the real promise: not just measurement, but momentum.

The Tipping Point: Real-Time Becomes Real Life

Then came the cascade:

- Dexcom G4 (2012): Sharper readings, more accuracy.
- Abbott's FreeStyle Libre (2014): No calibration, swipe-to-read.
- Dexcom G6 (2018): No fingersticks. Smartphone integration.
- Libre 3 and G7 (2023): Sleeker, faster, even more discreet.

Suddenly, people could:

- See their glucose every 5 minutes.
- Know whether they were rising or falling.
- Get alerts before they hit danger zones.
- Share their data with doctors or family across continents.
- Track the impact of food, stress, sleep—in real time.

This wasn't just a technological shift.

It was a psychological liberation.

Prediction becomes the New Prevention

In The Tipping Point, Gladwell wrote about connectors—people who link different worlds.

CGMs are connectors too. They link biology and behavior, emotion and algorithm, the past and the possible.

Because now, CGMs don't just monitor.

They predict.

They feed data into insulin pumps, closed-loop systems, mobile apps with machine learning.

They know what your glucose will be in 30 minutes—even if you don't.

They let you act before your body reacts.

That's no longer management.

That's forecasting.

That's foresight.

The Real Story isn't the Device

Here's the twist.

The story of CGM isn't really about glucose.

It's about control.

It's about taking a condition that was once silent, hidden, mysterious—and making it visible, audible, tangible.

It's about turning a chronic disease from something that happened to you… into something you can dance with.

CGMs didn't eliminate diabetes.

But they changed the conversation from reaction to anticipation.

And in the quiet between alerts and trends and charts, they gave people the most underrated medicine of all:

A sense that they were no longer alone.

Dexcom's Marketing Transformation—Partnering with Athletes and Influencers, and Real-time Dashboards

The Dashboard, the Athlete, and the Invisible Condition

Dexcom's Real-Time Marketing Leap

Every revolution has its symbols.

For some, it's a flag.

For others, a protest.

For Dexcom? It was a Super Bowl ad… and a rock star.

Not a metaphorical rock star.

An actual one: Nick Jonas.

The Boy Next Door with a Sensor on his Arm

When Dexcom launched its 2021 Super Bowl commercial featuring Jonas—a young, good-looking, healthy, and extremely public Type 1 diabetic—it wasn't selling just a product.

It was selling a new narrative.

Until then, diabetes marketing had looked remarkably the same:

A smiling senior citizen. A concerned mother.

A food chart. A lancet.

But Jonas didn't fit the mold.

He wasn't just a celebrity.

He was a data-driven diabetic.

He used Dexcom the way athletes use performance wearables.

His blood sugar wasn't a problem.

It was a metric. A challenge. A stat.

That commercial wasn't about glucose.

It was about empowerment.

And just like that, the invisible condition became a badge.

From Silent to Stylish

This was Dexcom's tipping point—not in technology, but in perception.

They made diabetes visible without shame.

They replaced the anxiety of numbers with the agency of dashboards.

They reframed management from compliance to optimization.

Athletes began talking.

Dexcom sponsored triathletes, Olympians, and endurance cyclists with Type 1 diabetes—not as exceptions, but as exemplars.

These weren't patients.

They were warriors with wearables.

The Influence Equation

Connectors are those rare individuals who tie disparate social worlds together.

Dexcom's move into influencer marketing wasn't just about reach.

It was about finding connectors who bridged two powerful communities:

- The chronic illness community—who live with diabetes every single day.
- The quantified self movement—who track every calorie, heartbeat, and REM cycle.

By partnering with lifestyle influencers, tech reviewers, and even fitness YouTubers, Dexcom positioned CGM not just as a medical tool, but as a life-performance device.

Wearing a Dexcom became no different than wearing a Fitbit or an Oura Ring—except now the stakes were higher, and the feedback was literal life data.

The Real-Time Dashboard: From Glucose to Storytelling

But the real secret weapon wasn't Nick Jonas.

It was the data dashboard.

Because once users saw their numbers not as abstract digits but as arcs, trends, and behaviors, everything changed.

- Spikes weren't just meals. They were habits.
- Lows weren't just bad luck. They were missed signals.
- Patterns weren't static. They were personalized narratives—changing daily.

Dexcom turned raw data into storytelling.

And humans—more than anything—respond to stories.

The Twist

In Blink, Gladwell talked about the power of thin-slicing—how rapid cognition shapes our perception in an instant.

Dexcom figured that out too.

Their marketing sliced through decades of inertia with a single visual:

A healthy, energetic person—glancing at their smartwatch—making a decision.

No finger-prick.

No pain.

No stigma.

Just insight.

And that glance, that blink, was worth more than any brochure.

It said:

“This is not your parents 'diabetes. This is yours.

You don't just live with it.

You master it.”

Not Just a Device. A Movement.

So yes, Dexcom sells sensors.

But what it really markets is sovereignty.

Over your condition.

Over your habits.

Over your fear.

And in doing so, it joins a lineage of quiet revolutions:

Where feedback becomes freedom.

And wearables become weapons of self-awareness.

Chapter 9

Novartis and Proteus Digital Health

The Pill that Texts You Back

How Novartis and Proteus Tried to Make Ingesting Medicine a Two-Way Conversation

Let's begin with something utterly unremarkable.

A pill.

Small. Coated. Swallowed in seconds.

It disappears into the body, into the bloodstream, into silence.

Now imagine if that pill could talk.

Imagine if, after you took it, it sent a tiny message—like a whisper from your stomach—that said, "I'm here. Mission accomplished."

That was the idea.

That was the vision.

That was the Proteus chip.

And for a moment, it looked like it might change everything.

The Missed Dose Problem

If you want to understand why a company like Novartis, a pharmaceutical juggernaut, would partner with a little Silicon Valley startup named Proteus Digital Health, you have to start with a very human, very old problem:

People forget to take their medicine.

Not some people.

Not sometimes.

Across chronic conditions, adherence rates average just 50%.

Half the time, the drug never meets the disease.

Now think like a pharmaceutical executive.

You've poured billions into R&D, regulation, distribution.

And then, your drug's effectiveness is compromised by forgetfulness?

That's not just frustrating.

That's existential.

Enter Proteus.

A Grain of Sand with a Purpose

Proteus created something magical: a sensor the size of a grain of sand, embedded into a pill, powered by stomach fluid. No battery. No wires.

Once swallowed, it activated, transmitted a signal to a patch worn on the skin, which then sent data to a smartphone app.

The pill had gone from silent to sentient.

It could now confirm ingestion.

Track heart rate.

Monitor rest and activity.

Alert caregivers.

For the first time in history, taking a pill became a data event.

Novartis Sees the Signal

This wasn't lost on Novartis.

In 2010, it announced a partnership with Proteus to embed this technology in organ transplant medications—where missing a single dose could mean rejection. The stakes couldn't be higher.

The pharmaceutical industry, often accused of moving slowly, suddenly seemed to be leaping into science fiction.

A drug company wasn't just providing treatment—it was now tracking trust, monitoring behavior, closing the loop.

It was moving from chemical to cybernetic.

The Twist: Trust is the Real Medicine

But this story isn't just about technology.

It's about psychology.

Because as it turns out, patients didn't just want to be healed.

They wanted to be trusted.

Some found the idea of a pill that reports on them… unsettling.

Others found it empowering.

And here lies the paradox:

The same technology that monitors can also motivate.

The same data that tracks can also transform.

For patients who forget doses, this was a lifesaver.

For caregivers, it was peace of mind.

For pharma, it was proof.

But for critics, it felt like surveillance.

A slippery slope from adherence to intrusion.

What Happened Next?

The Novartis-Protues collaboration showed early promise.

But then, reality:

- Technical challenges.
- Regulatory hurdles.
- Privacy questions.
- Reimbursement dilemmas.
- And a simple truth: behavior is harder to change than biology.

While Novartis eventually stepped back, Proteus continued its journey.

It partnered with Otsuka to develop Abilify MyCite, the world's first FDA-approved digital pill for schizophrenia.

It filed for bankruptcy in 2020.

Then resurfaced with new leadership and restructured vision.

The dream didn't die.

It morphed.

More than a Pill. A Philosophy.

Remember that success isn't just about talent, but timing, culture, legacy.

Proteus and Novartis had the talent.

Maybe they were early.

Maybe the culture wasn't ready.

But they asked a question that refuses to go away:

What if medicine wasn't just prescribed—but also heard, understood, responded to?

That question has spawned an entire movement—of digital therapeutics, smart devices, companion apps, behavioral nudges, AI adherence models.

Proteus lit a spark.

And now, a dozen others are chasing the fire.

In the End, a Pill That Texts You Back Is Really a Story of Listening

Not just to patients 'biochemistry.

But to their lives.

Their forgetfulness.

Their fears.

Their rhythms.

It's the story of two companies—one ancient, one audacious—trying to bridge the chasm between taking medicine and being well.

And in doing so, they revealed something essential:

That even in pharma, what you measure isn't as important as why you care.

The Rise and Fall of One of the Most Ambitious Digital Pill Ventures

The Pill that Dreamed Too Big

The Rise and Fall of Proteus Digital Health

Let me tell you a story that starts with a whisper.

A whisper from inside your stomach.

Not metaphorically.

Literally.

A tiny chip—no bigger than a grain of sand—swallowed with your morning medication.

No batteries. No charging port.

Just an electrical spark, triggered by your gastric juices, sending a signal through your body to a patch on your skin.

The patch sends it to your phone.

And your phone says: "The pill has landed."

That was the dream of Proteus Digital Health.

And for a brief moment in the 2010s, that whisper was supposed to roar.

An Idea before its Time

Remember Malcolm Gladwell's The Tipping Point, where he wrote about how small things can make a big difference.

Proteus was a small company with a very big idea:

To close the loop between taking medicine and knowing medicine was taken.

It wasn't the pill that changed.

It was the relationship.

Suddenly, a drug wasn't just ingested.

It was tracked.

Logged.

Verified.

Connected to a living stream of data.

And in a healthcare system bleeding billions from poor adherence and fragmented care, this seemed revolutionary.

A Who's who of Believers

And like any revolution, it attracted believers.

- Novartis signed on to test Proteus's sensor with transplant medications.
- Otsuka partnered to develop Abilify MyCite, the first FDA-approved digital pill for schizophrenia.
- $500 million in funding came pouring in from blue-chip investors, including Oracle, Medtronic, Novartis, and Kaiser Permanente.

In Silicon Valley, where moonshots are currency, Proteus seemed like a sure bet.

This wasn't just wearable tech—it was swallowable tech.

You couldn't get more intimate.

The Power of Feedback

Remember: Gladwell told us in Blink that that decisions made in the blink of an eye are often more accurate than those made with exhaustive analysis.

Proteus was selling the blink.

The instant feedback.

The loop closed.

The behavior reinforced.

It promised what medicine had always wanted but never dared ask for:

Certainty.

You didn't have to wonder if the patient took the pill.

The pill would tell you.

Then, the Silence

But then something strange happened.

The whisper stopped being inspiring.

It became unsettling.

Some patients felt surveilled.

Some providers didn't want the liability.

Some insurers refused to pay for pills that cost 10x more—just because they could talk.

And behind the scenes, the technology wasn't perfect.

Patches failed.

Apps crashed.

Signals dropped.

It's one thing to promise feedback.

It's another to build a feedback system that works flawlessly, every time, for everyone, inside the human body.

The science was elegant.

The execution was… human.

The Fall

In July 2020, Proteus filed for bankruptcy.

It had burned through hundreds of millions.

Partnerships faded.

The CEO stepped down.

The patents—once the crown jewels—were sold off quietly.

Proteus, once the shining hope of digital medicine, had now become a cautionary tale.

And just like that, the chip that dreamed of changing healthcare was swallowed by the system it tried to fix.

But did it Really Fail?

Maybe it is time to squint.

Because maybe this isn't a story of failure.

Maybe it's the "Howard Head" story of healthcare.

Howard Head was an engineer who failed to create a better ski, then failed to create a better tennis racket—until Wilson picked up his design and changed the sport.

Proteus may have failed as a company.

But it succeeded as a conceptual pivot point.

Today:

- Abilify MyCite still exists.
- Other companies are working on ingestibles, implantables, and smart drugs.
- Digital therapeutics are mainstream.
- The conversation has shifted from compliance to connected care.

Proteus didn't win the race.

But it mapped the terrain.

The Echo

Gladwell reminds us in his book, David and Goliath, that sometimes disadvantages are advantages in disguise.

Proteus faced a Goliath: medicine's inertia.

But in trying to fell it, they left behind a new vocabulary:

Digital pill.

Ingestible sensor.

Data-driven adherence.

Words that didn't exist before.

Ideas that can't be un-thought.

Their whisper became an echo.

And the industry is still listening.

Lessons in Overpromise, Privacy, and Market Readiness

The Mirage Effect

There's a story that venture capitalists love to tell themselves. It goes like this: "If you build something 10x better, the world will adopt it."

If it's more efficient, more connected, more measurable — it will win.

But what if that belief… is wrong?

What if the world doesn't adopt better?

What if the world resists it?

What if the world isn't waiting for a perfect solution — but one that feels right?

Welcome to the Proteus Paradox:

A story not just of innovation, but of timing, trust, and the subtle social calculus that technology often forgets to solve.

1. **Overpromise: The Romance of the Perfect Pill**

   In The Tipping Point, Gladwell wrote about how ideas spread like epidemics — they need stickiness, context, and carriers.

   Proteus had all three:

   A sticky idea: A pill that texts you back.

   A powerful context: a crisis in medication non-adherence.

   Charismatic carriers: Novartis, Otsuka, Silicon Valley's finest.

   And yet… it stalled.

   Why?

   Because promising a revolution is easy.

   Delivering a reliable, scalable, human-compatible version of that revolution is not.

   Proteus promised certainty, but delivered complexity:

- A smart pill that needed a patch, a phone, an app, and a cloud connection.
- A seamless loop… that often had friction.

The result?

The dream outpaced the infrastructure.

And when dreams move faster than reliability, disappointment compounds faster than progress.

2. Privacy: The Phantom Line We're Always Crossing

Proteus's sensor didn't just know you took your medication.

It knew when, where, how often, and maybe — how honestly.

And here's where things got tricky.

"Is it medicine… or surveillance?"

One patient's empowerment is another's intrusion.

One caregiver's peace of mind is another's control mechanism.

And in that ambiguity, Proteus underestimated something profound:

Privacy isn't about data. It's about perception.

It's about the story people tell themselves about who's watching, why, and what they'll do with the information.

People make decisions based on instinct as much as analysis.

Instinct said: This feels like someone is watching me from the inside out.

And for many patients, that instinct was enough to say no.

3. Market Readiness: The Idea That Arrived Before Its Time

Imagine trying to launch an iPhone in 1995.

No app stores. No 4G. No WiFi. No trust.

That's what Proteus was trying to do.

They offered a 21st-century solution to a healthcare system still stuck in the 20th.

- Regulators didn't know how to classify it.
- Insurers didn't know how to price it.

- Doctors didn't know how to integrate it.
- Patients didn't know how to feel about it.

Proteus didn't just build a new product.

It tried to create a new behavior.

And behaviors don't shift on schedule.

The Twist: The Mirage is Still Real

But here's the thing:

Just because you chase a mirage doesn't mean the water isn't coming.

Proteus failed.

But today:

- Wearables are mainstream.
- Digital therapeutics are reimbursed.
- Remote monitoring is routine.
- Trust in connected care is rising.

They weren't wrong.

They were just early.

Like Friendster before Facebook.

Like Newton before the iPhone.

Like Da Vinci sketching flying machines centuries before Boeing.

Three Final Lessons — Not Just for Startups, But for Storytellers

1. Never mistake technological possibility for psychological readiness. What works in code must also work in culture.
2. Privacy isn't binary. It's a dance between usefulness and comfort — a shifting boundary we navigate by feel, not fact.
3. Promise less magic. Deliver more meaning.People don't want to be dazzled.

They want to be understood.

In the end, Proteus didn't just teach us how to build a smarter pill.

It taught us something subtler:

That revolutionary ideas must first pass through the narrow door of human habit.

And until they do, even the smartest pill in the world… is hard to swallow.

Chapter 10

Fitbit + Pharma: From Step Counting to Strategic Partnerships

From Step Counting to Strategic Partnerships

In 2007, two Stanford alums set out to make a gadget that could count your steps. That was it.

No grand vision for transforming healthcare.

No aspiration to reshape pharma's relationship with patients.

Just a clip-on device to remind you to walk more.

It was called Fitbit.

Seventeen years later, that same device—now nestled on millions of wrists—had become something else entirely:

- A behavioral coach,
- A biometric data generator,
- A research assistant,
- And eventually, a bridge between pharma and the patient's body.

This chapter isn't just about how Fitbit evolved.

It's about how the idea of "fitness" expanded, and how a step-counting gadget became a vehicle for reimagining pharma marketing, clinical trials, and human engagement.

The 10,000 Step Fallacy and the Power of Suggestion

Let's begin with a number: 10,000.

For years, 10,000 steps was gospel.

Fitness guides swore by it. Doctors repeated it. The media amplified it.

But the number wasn't born in a lab.

It was born in 1965, in Japan, from a marketing campaign.

A pedometer called manpo-kei—meaning "10,000 step meter"—simply sounded good.

There was no science behind it.

It was a stickiness factor.

And yet—it worked.

Because it was simple.

And simplicity, when repeated enough, becomes ritual.

Fitbit: A Behavior Platform in Disguise

The early Fitbits were just toys.

Count your steps. Win a badge. Beat your friend.

But something was happening underneath:

People began changing their behavior—not because a doctor told them to, but because their wrist vibrated.

They walked longer to close their circle.

They skipped dessert to beat yesterday's calorie count.

They went to sleep early because a glowing ring told them they were "in recovery mode."

Behavioral science had found its Trojan horse.

And pharmaceutical companies took notice.

The Pivot: From Consumer Device to Clinical Tool

Here's a twist:

The story of Fitbit's transformation didn't start in a boardroom.

It started with researchers.

Academics began using Fitbits in small studies—on sleep, on exercise, on obesity.

Suddenly, they had real-time data.

No guesswork. No recall bias. Just continuous, passive, honest data.

Then something bigger happened.

In 2017, Fitbit announced a partnership with pharma giants like Pfizer, Biogen, and Bristol-Myers Squibb.

The goal?

To see if Fitbit could detect atrial fibrillation.

Not just count steps—but predict stroke risk.

Suddenly, Fitbit wasn't just a gadget.

It was a diagnostic ally.

Why Pharma Leaned in?

Pharma's biggest challenge isn't always the pill.

- It's what happens before and after the pill.
- How do we find the right patients?
- How do we ensure they adhere?
- How do we prove outcomes, especially for value-based contracts?

Fitbit answered all three.

- Recruitment: Wearables helped identify eligible patients based on activity, sleep, or heart rate trends.
- Engagement: Real-time nudges kept users compliant.
- Evidence: Continuous data turned subjective health into objective metrics.

Suddenly, a step became a signal.

And a signal became a strategy.

The Real-World Case: Bristol-Myers Squibb & Fitbit for Atrial Fibrillation

In 2019, BMS, Pfizer, Fitbit, and the American Heart Association launched a joint initiative.

The aim?

To raise awareness—and eventually enable detection—of AFib, a leading cause of stroke.

Fitbit devices with optical heart rate monitors could flag irregular rhythms.

Users were prompted to seek medical attention.

Some did.

Lives were saved.

This wasn't a marketing campaign.

This was marketing that mattered.

Pharma wasn't selling.

It was participating.

Data as Destiny

Remember: Connectors are people who link different worlds.

Fitbit became a connector between the consumer world and the clinical world.

It taught pharma three things:

- Data is behavior. And behavior is health.
- Engagement isn't compliance. It's conversation.
- The future of medicine may live on a wrist. Not in a vial.

Google, Fitbit, and the Future of Connected Pharma

When Google acquired Fitbit in 2021, many feared the end of neutrality.

Would it become another ad platform?

Another data mine?

But for pharma, the implications were clear:

The biggest tech company now had access to real-time health behavior at global scale.

Clinical trials, patient segmentation, messaging strategies—all could now be personalized based on movement, sleep, heart rate, mood.

This wasn't just pharma marketing 2.0.

It was contextual medicine.

Final Thought: When Steps became Stories

Fitbit never set out to redefine healthcare.

It just wanted to make people move more.

But like many innovations, its users led the way.

They used it to sleep better, recover smarter, and manage chronic illness.

Pharma noticed.

And followed.

The story of Fitbit + Pharma is the story of what happens when a consumer device becomes a clinical ally, when data becomes destiny, and when your next prescription might begin with a gentle buzz on your wrist.

Not a pill.

Not a pamphlet.

Just a nudge.

And that, as we've seen before, is sometimes all it takes to start a revolution.

Case Studies of Fitbit's Collaborations with Pharma Companies Like Boehringer Ingelheim, Bristol-Myers Squibb, and Pfizer

When a Step becomes a Signal: Case Studies of Fitbit's Foray into Pharma

In the world of pharmaceutical marketing, there's a hidden variable rarely talked about in boardrooms: the moment before the symptom.

The flutter before the fibrillation.

The quiet breathlessness before the cough.

The one bad night of sleep that precedes a two-week slide into depression.

For centuries, these moments were invisible—lost in the noise of everyday life, unrecorded, and certainly unmarketed to.

But what if a wristwatch could see them?

What if pharma stopped waiting for the patient to arrive at the clinic—and instead showed up before the first symptom?

That is, in essence, what Fitbit began to do when it stopped being a gadget company and started becoming a bridge—between pharma, patient, and prediction.

Pfizer + Bristol-Myers Squibb + Fitbit: Catching a Stroke before it Starts

Let's start with atrial fibrillation—AFib.

It affects over 30 million people globally, and it's sneaky. It comes and goes. It doesn't hurt. It doesn't scream. It whispers.

And then, one day, it causes a stroke.

Now imagine you're Pfizer and Bristol-Myers Squibb. You co-market Eliquis, one of the world's leading blood thinners. You know your drug works. But you can't prescribe it if no one knows they're at risk.

Enter Fitbit.

In 2019, these two pharma giants partnered with Fitbit to launch the "Find Your Rhythm" campaign—a hybrid of public health awareness and real-time screening initiative.

Fitbit's wearables, which use optical heart rate sensors, can passively track signs of irregular rhythm—potentially indicating undiagnosed AFib.

The device didn't diagnose.

It nudged.

It whispered back.

Users were told: "This might be worth a conversation with your doctor."

And here's what's fascinating: millions took action.

Thousands discovered they were at risk.

Some were prescribed Eliquis.

But more importantly, they were seen.

Pharma, once distant and faceless, had stepped closer—not with a billboard, but with a beat.

Boehringer Ingelheim + Fitbit: Walking with COPD Patients

Chronic Obstructive Pulmonary Disease (COPD) is a slow thief.

It doesn't rob you all at once—it takes a little breath each day.

For Boehringer Ingelheim, makers of Spiriva and other respiratory therapies, managing COPD wasn't just about meds.

It was about motion.

Because motion—or its absence—is a vital sign.

In 2021, the company partnered with Fitbit to study whether daily step counts could serve as digital biomarkers for COPD severity.

They asked a simple question:

Could a decline in steps predict a worsening episode before the patient noticed?

They didn't just gather data—they watched patterns:

- Steps declined before exacerbations.
- Resting heart rate ticked up.
- Sleep became fragmented.

Together, this created a predictive signature—an early warning system.

This wasn't just about measuring disease.

It was about anticipating it.

Suddenly, pharma wasn't just reacting.

It was partnering with behavior.

It was listening.

And patients? They felt watched—but not surveilled.

They felt supported.

The watch wasn't scolding them.

It was keeping pace.

Behavioral Economics Meets Wearables: Nudges and the New Adherence

In all these partnerships, a new theme emerged:

Behavioral change doesn't begin with knowledge. It begins with a nudge.

The moment the wrist buzzes—"You've been sedentary for 90 minutes"—is the moment behavior tips.

Not because it's loud, but because it's personal.

Pharma learned that adherence wasn't about pillboxes or alarms—it was about momentum.

Fitbit offered that momentum—10,000 steps at a time.

Not Just Data—Narratives

What makes these collaborations so compelling isn't the hardware.

It's the human stories inside the data.

- The man in Chicago who discovered his AFib through a Fitbit, and now walks three miles a day on Eliquis.
- The woman in Frankfurt whose watch warned her of declining steps—prompting a Spiriva inhaler adjustment before her COPD flare.
- The rural patient who never saw a pulmonologist, but stayed out of the hospital because her wearable knew her patterns better than she did.

These are not marketing wins.

These are narrative wins.

And in pharma, a single story—when told with empathy and data—can redefine an entire brand.

Final Thought: From Measurement to Meaning

Fitbit's entry into pharma wasn't planned. It wasn't polished. It wasn't even obvious.

It happened the way tipping points always do:

- Slowly, then suddenly.
- Step by step.
- Buzz by buzz.

Because in the end, the most powerful thing a wearable does isn't just measure your body.

It tells your story—to you, to your doctor, and now, to your pharma partner.

And stories, as we've seen, change everything.

Using Wearables in R&D, Trials and Disease Awareness Campaigns

The Wristband and the Whisper: How Wearables Are Rewriting Research and Awareness in Pharma

Every scientific revolution begins not with a thunderclap, but with a question.

And in this case, the question was stunningly simple:

"What if the body could log its own experience—without a researcher present?"

For decades, pharmaceutical R&D followed a choreography so rigid it felt like theater:

Volunteers came into clinics. They filled out forms. They wore heart monitors—sometimes.

They described pain on a scale of 1 to 10. They recalled what they ate, how they slept, what they felt—in retrospect.

But the human body doesn't operate in retrospect.

It operates in real-time.

And that, it turns out, is where wearables changed everything.

From the Lab to the Living Room: The New R&D Frontier

Imagine this: A pharmaceutical company is conducting a trial for a Parkinson's drug.

In the old world, success depended on observation windows.

Once a month, the patient would visit the clinic.

Doctors would ask: "How are your tremors?"

And the patient—trying earnestly to remember—would say, "Not bad lately. A little worse in the morning."

Now imagine the same trial, except the patient wears a smartwatch equipped with motion sensors, tracking tremors continuously.

No need to remember.

No need to guess.

No need for approximation.

Suddenly, a disease defined by unpredictability has a pattern.

Suddenly, pharma has data at resolution previously unimaginable.

That's what Roche and Apple did.

That's what GSK and Propeller Health did with asthma sensors.

That's what hundreds of decentralized trials are now exploring across the world.

The lab didn't disappear.

It simply moved into your wrist.

The Invisible Epidemic: How Awareness Begins with a Notification?

Now let's shift scenes.

This time, the story begins not in a lab, but on a sidewalk.

A man is walking his dog. His watch vibrates.

A message flashes:

"You've had several irregular heart rhythms this week. This may be a sign of AFib. Please speak to your doctor."

This is not a clinical trial.

It's not even a diagnosis.

It's something far subtler—and more powerful.

It's awareness.

This is where pharma marketing enters the picture—not as the traditional megaphone, but as the quiet guide.

Take the "Find Your Rhythm" campaign by Pfizer, BMS, and Fitbit.

It wasn't about selling a drug.

It was about creating a moment of recognition—before a stroke, before a hospitalization, before it was too late.

In marketing, that's called a "conversion funnel."

In human life, it's called being seen.

The Pivot: Disease Awareness as Tipping Point

Remember the "stickiness factor?" That's what makes a message not just heard, but remembered and acted upon.

Wearables introduced a new kind of stickiness—not with words, but with data + context:

- "Your step count has dropped 22% over 3 weeks."
- "Your resting heart rate is up 8 BPM from your baseline."
- "Your blood oxygen dipped three nights in a row."

This wasn't advertising.

It was personalized prompting.

And pharma realized something profound:

The greatest awareness campaign isn't a billboard.

It's a behavioral mirror.

Wearables in Trials: The End of the Black Box

Let's return to R&D.

In traditional trials, dropout rates are notoriously high.

Data gaps are enormous.

Engagement is minimal.

But when participants wear a device that feeds back their own data—they stay involved.

They see progress.

They feel part of something.

The trial isn't being done to them.

It's being done with them.

Even more surprising?

Wearables have begun surfacing new endpoints.

Data scientists now notice:

- Mood changes linked to temperature fluctuations.
- Activity dips predicting depressive episodes.
- Nighttime heart rate variability correlating with drug side effects.

Suddenly, pharma isn't just proving efficacy.

It's discovering new dimensions of the disease.

And isn't that what science is supposed to do?

Not confirm what we already suspect—but show us what we never thought to ask?

The Closing Twist: From Wearables to Whisperables

Here's the final insightl:

Wearables, for all their hardware, aren't devices.

They are whispering systems.

They don't shout.

They don't sell.

They suggest, infer, reveal.

And in both clinical trials and public health messaging, that whisper is enough to tip behavior, to reshape self-perception, and to bring pharma closer to the pulse of life—literally.

Because in the end, it's not about the steps.

It's about the story the steps tell.

And that story is just beginning to be heard.

Chapter 11

Wearables in Oncology Trials – The Takeda Experience

The Side Effect that Spoke First

How Takeda Gave Cancer Patients Their Data—and Their Dignity—Back

In the old model of oncology trials, patients came in, filled out forms, and left. Their experience—the fatigue, the nausea, the sleep disruptions—was documented by the physician, not the patient. A doctor would summarize it all in a code, a line item: "Grade 2 adverse event. Moderate."

But cancer doesn't show up as bullet points.

It shows up as missed dinners.

As walks cut short.

As nights without sleep.

And for Takeda, one of the world's leading oncology players, this discrepancy became a question too big to ignore:

"What if the most important part of the trial is happening between visits?"

When Cancer Went Home—and the Data Followed

The moment arrived quietly.

Takeda began placing wearable devices—think Fitbits, smartwatches, sleep bands—on the wrists of oncology patients not just to track movement, but to listen to life.

Because here's the twist: in cancer trials, sometimes the drug works…

but the patient can't feel it.

And other times, the patient feels it before the labs confirm it.

Traditional endpoints—tumor shrinkage, progression-free survival—are cold.

What Takeda wanted was warm:

- Steps taken.
- Sleep patterns.
- Skin temperature.
- Circadian rhythm disruptions.

It was the first attempt to digitize something medicine had always struggled to quantify:

"How are you feeling, really?"

The Flip: Passive Data as Active Voice

In The Tipping Point, Gladwell discussed how small things—such as the hushed advice of a trusted friend—could spark an epidemic of change.

Wearables in oncology didn't announce themselves.

They didn't beep, ping, or lecture.

They sat silently on the skin… and recorded truths patients never reported.

One patient in the trial had told her doctor she was "doing okay."

But her wearable told a different story:

- 70% reduction in steps.
- Heart rate variability dropping.
- Sleep reduced to 3 fragmented hours per night.

She wasn't fine.

She was exhausted, borderline collapsing, and too proud to say so.

That changed everything.

When Patients became Partners

Here's the real shift: these devices didn't just collect data—they changed dynamics.

Patients no longer felt like subjects.

They were now co-pilots in their own treatment journey.

- They could see their daily patterns.
- They could flag changes before the next appointment.
- They could connect dots their oncologists hadn't considered.

In return, Takeda didn't just get better data.

They got earlier warnings.

They could adjust doses, prevent dropouts, and in some cases, save lives.

All because the body whispered… and someone finally listened.

The Science behind the Empathy

But make no mistake: this wasn't just about compassion.

This was data at scale.

Takeda's digital trials began to reveal:

- Patterns between sleep fragmentation and toxicity onset
- Correlations between mobility decline and neutropenia episodes
- Digital biomarkers that predicted side effects days before lab results

It was the beginning of predictive oncology—not with MRI scans, but with steps, snores, and stillness.

The Cultural Challenge: From Gut Feelings to Graphs

But here's where the story gets complicated.

Some oncologists were skeptical.

How could step counts possibly rival imaging?

And yet, the data didn't lie.

Patients who showed early wearable-reported distress had 30% higher trial dropout rates.

Those who maintained circadian regularity responded better to chemo.

The trend line had become a storyteller.

The Epilogue: Quiet Technology, Loud Impact

So what did Takeda learn?

That the future of cancer research may not lie in more aggressive drugs…

but in more attentive listening.

Wearables gave voice to what had always been silent:

- The slow erosion of vitality
- The small daily wins
- The moments of despair between hospital visits

This wasn't just a tech story.

It was a human story.

Because in a disease that takes so much, wearables gave patients something back:

Their data, yes.

But also their dignity.

Takeda's Use of Wearable Patches and Biosensors to Track Fatigue, Pain, and HRV

When the Body Told the Truth

How Takeda Used Skin-Deep Tech to Uncover Deeper Signals in Cancer Care

There's a curious thing that happens in medicine.

We ask patients how they're feeling—

and then proceed to ignore everything that can't be measured.

Pain? Subjective.

Fatigue? Elusive.

Sleep disturbances? Vague.

For decades, oncologists built billion-dollar treatments to shrink tumors.

But when it came to how people actually lived with cancer, they relied on a shrug and a checkbox.

Until Takeda did something unusual.

They stopped asking.

And started listening—through the skin.

The Patch that knew more than the Patient Said

In Blink, Gladwell wrote that people often make snap judgments based on unconscious data—tiny signals they can't even articulate. The same, it turns out, is true of the body itself.

Takeda's team began using wearable patches that adhered quietly to patients 'skin.

No screens. No buzzing. No buttons.

Just a sensor, silently recording:

- Heart Rate Variability (HRV): the microscopic variation between heartbeats
- Skin temperature
- Galvanic skin response
- Motion data—not just how much someone moved, but how they moved

In those little signals—flickers most people can't feel—Takeda found what the questionnaires had missed:

A dip in HRV before the patient reported nausea.

A drop in activity before fatigue was mentioned.

Micro-tremors that preceded full-blown neuropathy.

The patch was no longer just a device.

It was a translator between the body and the care team.

The Invisible Made Visible

Pain is a funny thing.

It shows up first in your gait, in your posture, in how long you hesitate before getting out of bed.

Takeda's biosensors started seeing pain before it was spoken.

They noticed patterns:

- When HRV dropped and temperature spiked, pain was likely escalating.
- When movement slowed but wasn't accompanied by sleep, something was wrong.
- When a patient tossed and turned for three nights in a row, it wasn't "insomnia"—it was distress.

This was thin-slicing at a molecular level.

Just as seasoned art experts can spot a forgery in an instant, Takeda's algorithmic engines began picking up the quiet signals of suffering.

Redesigning the Trial Around the Patient's Body Clock

Traditionally, clinical trials are built around schedules.

Visit on Day 1. Dose on Day 14. Report on Day 28.

But the body doesn't follow protocol. It pulses to its own rhythm.

Takeda's patches turned clinical trials into dynamic feedback systems:

- Dosing windows adjusted based on real-time fatigue levels
- Adverse events flagged days earlier than standard practice
- Digital dashboards that showed not just "response" or "relapse," but resilience

For the first time, oncology trials weren't just measuring tumor regression.

They were measuring the return of normal life.

When Data became Empathy

Here's the twist.

The most powerful outcome of Takeda's wearable strategy wasn't statistical.

It was emotional.

Patients began to say:

"I feel like they're finally seeing what I go through."

"I don't have to explain—I just wear the patch."

"They know when I'm struggling before I even know it."

In David and Goliath, Gladwell explores the idea that perceived weaknesses can become strengths.

Takeda flipped the script on fatigue—a nebulous complaint, long dismissed—and turned it into a primary endpoint.

Suddenly, how tired you felt was no longer a side note.

It was the story.

Final Thought: What the Skin Always Knew

In the end, Takeda didn't just improve cancer trials.

They redefined what counted as evidence.

- Not just CT scans, but circadian patterns
- Not just symptom diaries, but electrodermal whispers
- Not just endpoints, but the lived experience of being sick

Because the body is always speaking.

It's just that for most of medical history, no one was listening.

Until a patch was placed on the skin.

And the data—finally—spoke for the patient.

A Revolution in Subjective Endpoint Measurement

The Metric You Couldn't Measure

How Medicine Finally Began to Believe the Patient

There's a moment in every scientific revolution where someone asks a question that sounds almost absurd.

In the case of modern clinical research, the question was this:

"What if how the patient feels is just as important as what the lab shows?"

For most of medical history, that wasn't science.

It was soft.

Unreliable.

Subjective.

Symptoms like fatigue, anxiety, pain, or sadness were anecdotal, filtered through messy human memory and biased interpretation.

But then something changed.

Not with a discovery, but with a decision:

To start measuring the unmeasurable.

From Hard Endpoints to Human Experiences

In clinical trials, we've always trusted the "hard endpoints":

- Blood pressure.
- Tumor size.
- Cholesterol levels.
- Mortality rates.

These were clean, quantifiable, statistically significant.

Meanwhile, a patient's dizziness, sleep trouble, or sense of well-being was noted like background noise—if at all.

But as wearables, biosensors, and AI tools advanced, something remarkable happened:

Subjective endpoints became observable.

And once they were observable, they became trustworthy.

And once they were trustworthy, they began to reshape everything.

The Tipping Point

Think of it like this:

In the Tipping Point, Gladwell described how ideas spread like viruses—through connectors, mavens, and the stickiness of small things.

Subjective data followed a similar path.

One pharma company began to track mood via wearables.

Another integrated real-time fatigue score is incorporated into cancer dosing.

Another used AI facial recognition to monitor distress.

These weren't just gadgets—they were listening devices for the body's inner story.

And before long, a quiet consensus began to form:

"If we don't measure what matters to patients, we're measuring the wrong things."

The Revolt of the Patient-Reported Outcome

The revolution had a name:

PROs—Patient Reported Outcomes.

But it wasn't the questionnaire that changed everything.

It was the context.

- When PROs were tied to biometric sensors, they became verifiable.
- When subjective reports correlated with relapse patterns, they became predictive.
- When digital therapeutics adapted to emotional states, they became prescriptive.

Suddenly, how someone felt wasn't just noise in the system—it was a signal.

A Case Study in Empathy Engineering

Consider this: in one oncology trial, patients wore a patch that tracked their heart rate variability and sleep disruption.

Those who reported "feeling exhausted" weren't taken at their word.

Until the data aligned.

Their fatigue wasn't laziness.

It was a measurable shift in circadian rhythm, autonomic stress, and metabolic load.

It was the difference between dropping out and finishing the trial.

A subjective endpoint, once dismissed, became the canary in the coal mine.

The Scientist who Listened Differently

Every revolution has its iconoclasts.

In this case, they weren't radical.

They were researchers who simply asked:

"What if our most powerful data comes from the inside out?"

They were behavioral psychologists, UX designers, biomedical engineers—people who knew that how we feel is not secondary.

It's central.

And they reimagined endpoints not as numbers on a spreadsheet…

but as narratives.

Stories of how patients eat, sleep, walk, think, move, ache, and hope.

The Quiet Ending: A New Kind of Certainty

What began as a whisper is now a movement.

Regulators are recognizing digital biomarkers of subjective states.

Pharma companies are investing in empathy metrics.

Patients are wearing devices that turn emotion into evidence.

And clinical trials are evolving from tests of drugs

to partnerships in well-being.

Because in the end, what's more real:

- The millimeter a tumor shrinks?
- Or the moment a patient finally sleeps through the night?

The revolution in subjective endpoint measurement didn't make medicine softer.

It made it truer.

PART IV: WEARABLE STRATEGY FOR PHARMA BRAND MANAGERS

Part IV

Wearable Strategy for Pharma Brand Managers

The Hidden Lever

How Pharma Brand Managers Found the Next Strategic Edge—on a Wrist, in a Patch, and Under the Skin

There's a story I love about the early days of advertising.

In 1929, Edward Bernays—nephew of Sigmund Freud—was asked by the American Tobacco Company how to make cigarettes more acceptable for women. So, on Easter Sunday, he staged a parade where suffragettes lit up "Torches of Freedom" in public. It wasn't about nicotine. It was about narrative.

And for the next century, branding in health was just that:

The art of telling the right story at the right time to the right person.

Until that story got a new co-author: data.

And not just any data—real-time, streaming, personal, physiological data pulled directly from the skin, the body, the breath.

Welcome to the wearable revolution.

Welcome to the new rulebook for pharmaceutical brand managers.

From Campaigns to Continuous Care

For generations, pharma marketers dealt in campaigns.

Seasonal spikes. One-time launches.

Detailing. Segmentation. Sampling.

But now, imagine this:

- You know which patient missed their morning dose—at 9:04 a.m.
- You know which population segment walked fewer steps this week—before their HbA1c levels rise.

- You know which oncologist opened the dashboard five times this week—searching for fatigue trends in their trial participants.

Suddenly, pharma isn't playing offense once a quarter.

It's engaged in micro-adjustments, in real time, every day.

And brand managers?

They're no longer product promoters.

They're health system architects.

The Tipping Point for Trust

Remember that little things can make a big difference—if they're sticky, contagious, and carried by the right messengers.

Wearables are that kind of tipping point.

They've moved from fitness toys to clinical tools.

From step counters to symptom forecasters.

From lifestyle data to life-saving insights.

For pharma brand managers, this is more than a new medium.

It's a new mandate:

"Be there when it matters—not just when the script is written."

A Strategy Shift: From Awareness to Adherence, from Reach to Relationship

The traditional marketing funnel—Awareness → Interest → Desire → Action—assumes distance.

But wearables shrink that space.

They dissolve the delay between insight and intervention.

Which means:

- Your brand isn't just a molecule.
- It's the nudge that improved sleep.
- It's the alert that caught early breathlessness.
- It's the visualization that empowered a patient to keep going.

When every heartbeat is data, and every dashboard is a dialogue, the best brand strategy isn't storytelling.

It's co-monitoring, co-managing, co-creating health.

What this Part of the Book Offers

In the pages that follow, we'll leave behind the lab and step into the boardroom.

You'll learn how to:

- Identify the right wearables for your therapeutic area
- Build value-driven partnerships with tech companies
- Design adherence and engagement strategies rooted in real-time feedback
- Use wearable data for segmentation, targeting, and brand differentiation
- Craft regulatory-smart campaigns that respect privacy but unlock personalization
- And perhaps most importantly, tell a story that patients want to live inside—not just read in a brochure.

Because wearables aren't just changing what patients do.

They're changing what they expect.

And the brand managers who thrive in this world won't just adapt.

They'll lead the pulse of a new kind of marketing.

One that listens.

One that responds.

One that wears its strategy on the skin.

Chapter 12

Reimagining Segmentation in a Wearable World

What Pharma Missed When it Forgot to Listen to the Body

In the early 1990s, a small grocery chain in the U.K. made a quiet shift.

Instead of sending out coupons by ZIP code, they used loyalty card data to track what customers actually bought. A woman who never purchased wine? They stopped mailing her wine promotions. Someone who bought diapers? They'd receive formula offers, then toys, and finally back-to-school flyers—years ahead of schedule.

It was the beginning of behavior-based segmentation.

And it changed retail forever.

Pharma is having its loyalty card moment—but the card is now a sensor.

The rewards? Real-time insights.

And the customer? No longer a passive patient, but a living, breathing, streaming source of truth.

The Old Segmentation Model: Neat Boxes, Messy People

For decades, pharma brand managers carved up their audience using familiar scalpels:

- Age
- Gender
- Socioeconomic status
- Prescriber decile
- Geography
- Comorbidities

They created personas and target lists, mapped customer journeys, and grouped physicians by specialty or prescribing patterns.

But here's the thing:

The human body doesn't behave in demographics.

A 58-year-old sedentary diabetic may move more, sleep better, and adhere more closely than a 40-year-old marathoner with asthma who never checks their inhaler tracker.

Traditional segmentation told us who the patient was.

Wearables tell us what they do.

And that's a very different kind of marketing truth.

A Segmentation Story: The Sleeper Problem

Take sleep.

Two patients. Same age. Same diagnosis. Same meds.

One sleeps like a baby.

The other tosses, turns, and wakes up groggy.

Before wearables, you'd never know.

Today, the data shouts:

This patient is headed for burnout. Non-adherence. A call to the ER.

And suddenly, your segment isn't just "Type 2 diabetics in urban India."

It's "Low-activity, poor-sleep, stress-flagged, medium-adherent patients who spike post-lunch."

This isn't segmentation.

It's situation-mapping.

It's person-as-pattern.

The Twist: Thin Slicing the Invisible

Think of the power of thin slicing—those subconscious, split-second decisions we make based on a sliver of data.

Now, imagine a brand manager with the ability to thin slice a population not from instinct…

…but from continuous data streams.

- Spikes in skin temperature?

→ Pre-fever segment.

- Missed morning med + low step count + rising HRV?

→" Red zone" non-adherence cluster.

- Consistently active but irregular sleep and logging?

→" Silent struggler" microsegment.

These patterns were always there—hidden under assumptions and averages.

Wearables make them visible.

And visibility breeds strategy.

Welcome to Bio-Behavioral Segmentation

It's not just what people say.

It's what their bodies whisper.

A new segmentation framework is emerging—call it:

Bio-behavioral segmentation

Powered by wearables. Shaped by context. Driven by real-time relevance.

Here, you don't segment by profile.

You segment by trajectory.

- Is this patient stabilizing or slipping?
- Is this HCP's cohort responding or resisting treatment changes?
- Is the population's movement, mood, or medication intake following a trend or an outlier pattern?

And your brand responds not with static assets…

…but with dynamic nudges, adaptive journeys, and hyperpersonalized interventions.

The Strategic Shift: From Static Lists to Living Maps

Imagine this.

Instead of a brand dashboard showing broad market segments, it lights up with:

- "46,392 patients moved from green to amber this week."
- "Top 10 prescribers seeing fatigue-linked adherence dip."
- "Opportunity: 12% of newly diagnosed patients in Region X are showing symptom flare before next visit."

This isn't the future.

It's what's possible now.

Because segmentation isn't just a planning tool anymore.

It's a live conversation between brand, body, and behavior.

The Takeaway

In the wearable era, segmentation is no longer about boxes.

It's about biomes.

It's about rhythms.

It's about movement, mood, sleep, struggle, and success—measured at the skin level, aggregated in the cloud, and activated at the speed of need.

Brand managers who embrace this shift won't just target better.

They'll care smarter, engage deeper, and create brand experiences that feel less like marketing and more like knowing.

And when that happens?

Segmentation won't be a spreadsheet anymore.

It'll be a story.

And stories, as we know, change everything.

From Demographics to Data-graphics: Segmenting by Behavior, Biosignals, and Biometric Profiles

How the Body Became the Message

Let's begin with something familiar.

Imagine two patients. Both are 54. Both are male. Both live in the same zip code. Both have hypertension.

Traditional marketing logic would tell you: they're in the same segment.

But one walks 10,000 steps a day, rarely skips medication, sleeps deeply, and meditates twice a week.

The other? He naps at odd hours, rarely moves past 2,000 steps, and his heart rate variability—if you bothered to measure it—is as jittery as a leaf in a thunderstorm.

On paper, they're identical.

On wearables, they're worlds apart.

The Demographic Mirage

For decades, demographics were the map.

Age. Gender. Income. Education. Region.

It made sense in a world where data was scarce and broad strokes sufficed.

But the assumption baked into demographics was simple:

People like you behave like you.

That was the lie.

Because as it turns out, behavior doesn't respect boundaries.

A 70-year-old yoga teacher in Kerala might be more active than a 30-year-old desk worker in Bangalore.

A 45-year-old with asthma might sleep better than a 25-year-old night-shift ER nurse.

If the insight you need lives in the body…

…then why are you segmenting by the birthday?

Enter: The Biometric Storyline

The revolution isn't that we're collecting new data.

- It's that we're listening to new rhythms.
- Step count tells us about motivation.
- Sleep cycles tell us about mood.
- Skin temperature whispers inflammation.
- Heart rate variability flags emotional distress long before the face shows it.
- Medication ingestion sensors verify adherence without a word spoken.

Suddenly, segmentation isn't what people say—it's what their biosignals reveal.

This isn't just data.

This is a living narrative.

Thin Slices and Skin Signals

In Blink, Gladwell wrote about how a tennis coach could predict a double fault before the racket hit the ball. Not from technique—but from subtle cues, body signals, micro-tremors.

Wearables have brought this to pharma.

They let brand managers thin-slice a population—not based on who people are, but on how their bodies behave.

And behavior, unlike birthday or address, evolves.

Which means your segmentation must evolve with it.

From Buckets to Biometrics

Traditional segmentation felt like geography. You mapped the world into regions.

Biometric segmentation feels more like weather.

You don't group by landmass. You group by atmosphere:

- "Low activity, high inflammation" clusters.
- "Poor sleep + rising resting heart rate" microsegments.
- "Excellent adherence but rising anxiety metrics" trendlines.

It's fluid. It shifts weekly. It reacts to life.

And in this world, your job as a brand manager is no longer to draw boundaries…

…but to detect patterns.

The Data-graphic Future

We're entering the era of data-graphics—real-time, dynamic visualizations of human behavior and biology in motion.

Picture this:

- A dashboard where cohorts pulse in and out of alert zones.
- A color map where biosignal clusters light up like weather radars.
- A live segmentation feed: "15% of your users show signs of fatigue-induced nonadherence."
- A predictive nudge engine: "Target this subsegment with a sleep-optimization message. They're about to disengage."

Marketing meets medicine.

Engagement meets empathy.

Because what matters now is not how people look—but how they live.

The Takeaway

Demographics built pharma's past.

Data-graphics will shape its future.

Segmenting by behavior, biosignals, and biometric profiles means meeting the patient not where they reside, but where they are, how they feel, and what their body is telling you—before they ever say a word.

The most effective pharma marketers of tomorrow won't just market to a segment.

They'll converse with a pulse.

And the most meaningful message?

Will be the one timed precisely to when the data says: Now… they're ready to hear it.

Creating Dynamic Personas from Wearable Data

The Breathing Persona: How Wearable Data Breathed Life into Pharma's Target Audience

Back in the golden age of advertising, Don Draper didn't need data. He needed a hunch. He lit a cigarette, stared out a window, and told the world what it wanted.

Today? That hunch is wearing a smartwatch.

The Old Persona: A Cardboard Cutout

In marketing workshops around the world, there's a ritual.

It begins with a template:

- "Meet Anita, age 42, working mother, Type 2 diabetes, lives in Pune, tech-savvy."

Then come motivations, goals, frustrations—all based on interviews, surveys, maybe a focus group.

Anita is nice. She has a name, a stock photo, maybe even a quote in italics: *"I just want to stay healthy for my kids."*

But Anita, let's be honest, is a guess.

A well-reasoned fiction.

Because Anita may say she walks every day—but the wearable says she stopped three weeks ago.

She may say she's fine—but her HRV plummeted after her last clinic visit.

She may say she's engaged—but the data shows she hasn't opened her digital diary in ten days.

This is the chasm between static personas and living truth.

The New Persona: Streaming, Breathing, Becoming

Now imagine something different.

What if your "Anita" was:

- 8,432 steps today (1,200 fewer than usual)

- 5.2 hours of sleep (interrupted twice)
- Blood glucose variability up 14% since last weekend
- App engagement at 92% last week, now dipping
- Sentiment from text input: "I'm feeling overwhelmed lately."

This isn't a persona.

This is a pulse.

The Flip: From Archetype to Algorithm

In The Tipping Point, Gladwell explored how context shapes behavior. The person who helps a stranger on the street isn't necessarily kinder. Maybe they just weren't late.

Wearables give us context.

They show us Anita on Monday vs. Anita on Thursday.

They reveal her cycles, her dips, her silent triumphs.

And suddenly, your brand isn't marketing to an archetype.

It's engaging a moving target—with empathy, timing, and relevance.

Personas That Pivot

In a wearable-driven world, personas aren't static.

They:

- Update in real-time (Fatigue score fell? Push a nudge.)
- Adapt seasonally (Winter steps lower? Reinforce indoor activity tips.)
- Split into sub-cohorts (Same diagnosis, different behavioral clusters.)
- Anticipate need (Respiratory rate trending up? Time to talk prevention.)

You don't just build personas.

You listen to them breathe.

The Living Library

Every patient becomes a story. Not a case study.

A living chapter in a library that updates hourly.

As a brand manager, you no longer speak to "segments."

You speak to moods.

To movements.

To early signs and late fatigue.

To invisible decisions forming beneath the skin.

It's not about selling the drug.

It's about joining the journey.

The Takeaway

The greatest lie in marketing was that we knew our customers.

The greatest truth wearables revealed?

They knew themselves all along. We just needed to listen.

When you create dynamic personas from wearable data, you stop writing scripts…

and start responding to rhythms.

Because the next big campaign won't come from a whiteboard.

It'll come from a wrist.

Chapter 13

Hyperpersonalized Campaigns – Right Time, Right Signal, Right Message

Hyperpersonalized Campaigns: Right Time. Right Signal. Right Message.

In the 1960s, psychologist Walter Mischel devised a simple test involving children, a marshmallow, and a promise.

You could eat the marshmallow now.

Or wait 15 minutes, and get two.

What Mischel discovered wasn't just about willpower—it was about timing.

Some kids squirmed, others sang to distract themselves, and some cracked at 14 minutes and 50 seconds.

But the bigger truth was this: Behavior is a dance with time.

Fast forward to today, and the marshmallow has been replaced by medications, steps, alerts, and nudges.

But the question remains: When is the right moment?

And in the age of wearables, pharma might finally have the answer.

The Ticking Clock of Engagement

Imagine this:

A woman named Priya has just returned from work. Her heart rate is elevated, her skin temp up by half a degree. Her wearable knows she slept poorly the night before and skipped her afternoon walk. It's 8:47 PM, and her glucose levels are about to spike from that mango smoothie she always has post-dinner.

You're a brand manager with a Type 2 diabetes solution.

Traditional marketing would've sent her an SMS at 10 AM on a Wednesday.

But data-driven hyperpersonalization waits until now.

When the body is listening. When the mind is ready. When the moment can be changed.

So, the message reads:

"Hi Priya—gentle reminder: your body will thank you for a 10-minute walk after dinner tonight. Let's stabilize that curve."

That's not just marketing. That's a whisper between breath and behavior.

The Shift: From Campaigns to Conversations

In The Tipping Point, Gladwell wrote about how the smallest things—mavens, connectors, context—can ignite social epidemics.

Hyperpersonalized campaigns are the same.

They don't shout to the masses.

They speak precisely, almost whispering to an individual, at the exact intersection of physiology and psychology.

- Right time: Not Monday morning, but post-stress, pre-lapse.
- Right signal: Not demographic data, but a drop in heart rate variability or a missed dose.
- Right message: Not a general ad, but a behavioral nudge, shaped by biosignals and backed by empathy.

This is not automation.

It is anticipation.

The Science of Timing

Wearables taught us something remarkable:

Behavior is not just about what people do.

It's about when they're likely to change.

Take chronobiology—the science of body rhythms. Morning people respond better to alerts by 9 AM. Night owls? 10:45 PM.

Or micro-events: A spike in galvanic skin response might signal emotional distress. Pair that with declining app engagement, and you know the user is slipping.

Traditional marketing would've missed it.

Hyperpersonalized systems don't.

They time their entry like a jazz musician—never too early, never too late. Just right.

From Segments to Signals

Here's the radical idea: The segment is dead. The signal is king.

You don't market to "women aged 45–60 with hypertension."

You market to:

- Users with low HRV and rising resting heart rate.
- Patients who missed their medication 3 times in 6 days.
- Individuals whose wearables detect sleep disruption tied to chronic pain.

And the message?

It's no longer crafted in a boardroom.

It's sculpted by biosignal AI, behavioral science, and a deep respect for timing.

The Empathy Algorithm

Done right, hyperpersonalization doesn't feel like surveillance.

It feels like someone noticed.

- "You haven't walked much today—how about a quick stroll before bed?"
- "We noticed your heart rate went up during your doctor visit. Would you like to speak to a nurse?"
- "It's been 10 days since your last log-in. Everything okay?"

This isn't Big Brother.

It's a Big Brother Who Cares.

Case in Point: The 17% Rule

In a recent study, adherence improved by 17% when reminders were contextual, not scheduled.

The key?

- Not sending an alert at 8 PM sharp.

- Sending it at the first dip in HRV, post-meal, with a personalized message tied to last week's wearable insights.

It's like the message knew what the body was going through.

Because it did.

The Takeaway

Hyperpersonalized campaigns don't just "target."

They tune in.

They sense mood before behavior.

They whisper at the moment of need.

They shift the paradigm from mass outreach to molecular conversation.

Because in the end, the most effective message isn't the loudest or the cleverest.

It's the one that arrives like a friend,
right when you needed it,
just before you knew you did.

Contextual Marketing Using Biosensor Triggers

When the Body Speaks, and the Brand Listens

In 1999, researchers discovered something strange in a Las Vegas casino.

It wasn't about odds or jackpots, but how people responded to heat.

Gamblers who began to lose repeatedly—yet stayed at the table—shared one thing in common: a subtle rise in skin conductance. The more they lost, the sweatier their palms got. But—and here's the kicker—they weren't aware of it. Their bodies knew the risk before their brains caught up.

What if marketing could work the same way?

What if we didn't wait for people to say what they needed—

but instead, we listened to what their bodies were already saying?

That's the promise of contextual marketing powered by biosensor triggers.

The Whisper Beneath the Noise

You've likely heard of push notifications.

- "Time to take your medication."
- "Don't forget your evening walk."
- "Refill due in 2 days."

Useful? Sure. But they're reactive.

They speak in the language of timing, not context.

Now imagine this:

Emma, a 38-year-old with chronic migraines, is wearing a biosensor patch. On Tuesday at 4:43 PM, her wearable detects a slight uptick in her skin temperature, a subtle contraction in her trapezius muscles, and an increase in heart rate variability. These aren't random—they're pre-migraine signatures.

Ten minutes later, she gets this message:

"Emma, we noticed early signs of strain. Try five deep breaths. Would you like to start a 5-minute guided stretch?"

She hasn't even felt the migraine yet.

But the brand did.

And in that moment, the company isn't just a medication provider.

It becomes a lifeline.

The Law of Outlier Signal

In Blink, Gladwell wrote about how we often make snap decisions based on unconscious cues—tiny slivers of experience our brains process without telling us.

Contextual marketing turns that inward.

Instead of using past behavior to predict future need, it uses present biosignals to guide present action.

Heart rate.

Galvanic skin response.

Respiration.

Movement.

Sleep fragmentation.

Stress biomarkers.

These are not data points.

They are emotional breadcrumbs.

They are the body's way of whispering: "Something is about to change."

And in the split second before change arrives, contextual marketing steps in.

The Nudge, Refined

Let's say a Type 2 diabetes patient skips meals often.

The wearable detects an unexpected glucose dip—outside their normal rhythm.

Instead of a general alert, they receive:

"It looks like your glucose is lower than usual for this time of day. Consider a small healthy snack to stabilize energy."

It's not just personalized.

It's relevant to the moment.

It's contextual to the biology.

Now, layer in behavior science.

Send that message during a dopaminergic dip—say, after a long meeting or post-work fatigue—and the likelihood of action doubles.

This is precision empathy.

It's not about marketing louder.

It's about marketing closer.

The Smart Inhaler That Knew the Wind

Propeller Health once linked asthma inhalers to local weather data, air quality, and geolocation.

But what made it revolutionary?

The moment an asthmatic entered a high-risk air quality zone,

and their biosensor showed slightly labored breathing—it sent an alert to medicate proactively.

That's not marketing.

That's machine intuition.

Trust Built on Timing

We don't trust people because they show up.

We trust them because they show up at the right time.

Contextual marketing, driven by biosensor triggers, builds that trust by showing up:

- When stress starts, not when it's declared.
- When fatigue appears, not when it's complained about.
- When the body hesitates, not when the mind admits.

It's what separates a brand from a presence.

The Takeaway

Biosensor-triggered marketing doesn't guess.

It listens.

It's the difference between saying, "We know you," and saying, "We hear you."

Because the real breakthrough isn't in selling more.

It's in knowing when not to sell,

but simply to help.

And sometimes, that help arrives in the form of a soft vibration,

a well-timed nudge,

or a breath—just when you needed it most.

Before you even knew you did.

Real-world Scenario: Adjusting Reminders and Content Based on Heart Rate Variability (HRV) and Sleep Cycles

The Morning After: When the Algorithm Waits to Speak

A Real-World Scenario of HRV, Sleep, and Smart Nudges

At 7:03 a.m., Maya's alarm didn't go off.

But this wasn't a mistake.

It was a strategy.

You see, Maya, a 42-year-old clinical researcher managing two kids, a dog, and a chronic autoimmune condition, had worn a smart ring for the past six months. To her, it was a sleep tracker. To the pharmaceutical company supporting her wellness journey, it was something more: a barometer of readiness, a biological diary, and, occasionally, a guardian angel.

On this particular morning, the system detected two things:

- Her Heart Rate Variability (HRV) had dropped 22% overnight.
- Her REM sleep was fragmented, broken up by micro-wakes and restlessness.

Had you asked her, Maya would've shrugged it off. Just a normal bad night.

But the wearable knew better.

A Glitch in the Matrix, Not the Mind

Most people think of HRV as a cold metric, a beat-to-beat interval. But in reality, it's emotional. It's physiological poetry. A drop in HRV, paired with poor sleep, often means one thing:

The body is struggling to adapt to stress.

In Maya's case, it wasn't just sleep debt.

It was the beginning of a flare.

And here's where the magic happened.

The usual 7:00 a.m. push notification—"Time for your morning immune support med"—was held back.

Instead, at 8:12 a.m., after her ring sensed her cortisol spike had normalized and her HRV showed signs of recovery, Maya received this:

"Good morning, Maya. It seems like last night wasn't very restful. Consider a slower start today. Take your medication after breakfast, and here's a 3-minute breathwork session to get your system back in sync."

She tapped. Breathed. Paused. Smiled.

The New Language of Empathy

What happened wasn't just a scheduling adjustment.

It was contextual calibration.

It was marketing that whispered rather than shouted.

Because let's be honest: a poorly timed message—especially when you're exhausted—feels like spam.

But a message that aligns with your biorhythms?

That feels like care.

The Science behind the Kindness

The platform supporting Maya's regimen didn't just use sleep and HRV data for dashboards. It acted on them.

- It learned her circadian sweet spot—when her mood and clarity peaked.
- It studied her flare precursors—a mix of restless REM, early morning spikes, and irregular breathing.
- It knew her medication timing adherence, and how that correlated with symptom relief.

And then it did something extraordinary.

It waited.

That one-hour pause in messaging—based on her biological readiness—doubled her medication adherence that week. But more importantly, it built trust.

Maya didn't just take the pill.

She took it when she was most ready to hear the reminder.

What the Brand Learned

This wasn't about HRV or sleep alone.

It was about mood forecasting.

About finding the intersection of data and dignity.

And for the pharmaceutical brand behind the platform?

They didn't send more messages.

They sent fewer, but better.

They used wearables not to speak louder,

but to speak later, and softer—

at the moment it would matter most.

The Tipping Point

Maya wasn't just a user. She became an advocate.

Not because the medication changed.

But because the relationship did.

Her body spoke, and the brand listened.

And in that listening, trust bloomed.

Chapter 14

From Touchpoints to Touchwear

When the Message Moved from the Screen to the Skin

We used to think of marketing as a matter of moments.

The billboard you passed on your way to work.

The TV commercial between sitcoms.

The sales rep's visit to the physician's office.

These were the classic touchpoints—the places where brand and human intersected, briefly, and (hopefully) meaningfully.

They were engineered with great care.

They were choreographed to appear just in time.

But here's the thing:

Touchpoints were always external.

They happened to you.

Now, they happen with you.

Because something quietly revolutionary has arrived.

And it lives on your wrist, on your chest, or beneath your skin.

Welcome to the age of touchwear.

The Skin, the Signal, and the Story

A few years ago, a pharmaceutical brand launched a campaign around heart health. Their strategy was textbook:

- HCP materials at the clinic
- Animated explainer ads online
- Reminder emails around refill times

It was effective. But not transformative.

Then something changed.

They partnered with a smartwatch manufacturer. A subtle shift. No major ad blitz. Just a pilot.

But it changed everything.

Now, instead of an email three days before Maya's refill, the brand's digital assistant would wait for her heart rate to rise abnormally—a signal she typically sent the world after skipping a dose—and then gently tap her wrist.

The message?

"We noticed some changes. Need help staying on track?"

This wasn't a touchpoint.

It was touchwear.

It didn't interrupt. It interpreted.

It didn't declare. It dialogued.

And most importantly—it didn't just ask for attention.

It earned it.

The Inversion of Intimacy

Let's pause.

What made this shift so profound?

Remember ideas, behaviors, and messages spread like viruses when they're sticky, contagious, and land in fertile psychological ground.

Wearables create that ground.

They invert the logic of mass marketing.

Instead of asking: "How do we reach more people?"

They ask: "How do we understand the person better?"

Your wearable knows when you're anxious.

When you're still.

When you're sleep-deprived.

When your stress spikes just before your migraine does.

And so, the marketing doesn't just arrive on your screen.

It pulses through your environment, your timing, your mood—sometimes literally, as haptics on your wrist or light pulses on a patch.

It becomes behavioral choreography, not just communication.

The Death of the Funnel, The Rise of the Flow

The marketing funnel—awareness, interest, desire, action—was built for billboards and brochures.

But touchwear doesn't follow linear steps.

It follows biological rhythms.

Instead of:

Pushing a product…

It nudges a routine.

Instead of triggering fear…

It builds calm through consistency.

Instead of being campaign-based,

It becomes care-based.

This isn't storytelling.

It's body-listening.

From Clicks to Beats

Imagine a world where your engagement metric isn't a click-through rate, but a change in resting heart rate after a reassuring message.

Where your loyalty measure isn't prescription refill rates, but consistency in circadian alignment post-intervention.

Suddenly, marketing isn't a strategy.

It's a signal loop.

And your brand? It doesn't scream louder.

It learns better.

The Future: Invisible, Informed, Intuitive

In the coming decade, the most effective pharma brands won't be the ones with the loudest voice.

They'll be the ones with the lightest touch.

And that touch won't be on a banner ad or in a rep's brochure.

It will be:

- A skin-friendly patch that lights up when hydration dips.
- A nudge on the wrist that senses rising tension and suggests a breath.
- A glow on a wearable that says, "It's working. Keep going."

The message will not be delivered.

It will be felt.

The Last Touchpoint is You

What does it mean when marketing moves from medium to metabolism?

When the campaign is no longer separate from the body?

It means we've crossed a threshold.

From external persuasion to internal partnership.

From touchpoints to touchwear.

Rethinking Patient Journeys and Brand Interactions

Why the Waiting Room was never the Real Destination

In the traditional world of pharma marketing, the patient journey has long resembled a board game.

Start at symptom.

Roll the dice.

Land on diagnosis.

Draw a treatment card.

Advance to adherence.

Win by surviving side effects.

Pharma brand managers—well-meaning, data-driven, and eager—mapped this out like subway systems. Neat. Predictable. Linear. If the patient hesitated between stations? Add an awareness campaign. If they skipped their meds? Roll out a reminder app.

But what if that journey wasn't a map at all?

What if it were a river—winding, emotional, full of eddies and unexpected turns?

The Man who Forgot to Take his pills—and Why that Wasn't the Real Problem

Let me tell you about Calvin.

Calvin is 58. He has atrial fibrillation. His cardiologist prescribed him a novel anticoagulant—safe, effective, once-daily. For the first month, he was diligent. Then… something shifted.

The brand team flagged it as "non-compliance."

The algorithm referred to it as a "drop-off."

But the truth?

Calvin's granddaughter moved in.

She played the piano late into the night. Calvin stayed up listening. He began skipping his morning walk. He started waking up late. His smartwatch logged the change in circadian rhythm. His resting heart rate rose. But the system? Silent.

Until one day, Calvin felt dizzy. At the ER, the nurse asked: "Did you stop taking your meds?"

"No," he said, confused.

"I just stopped being myself for a while."

From Journey Maps to Emotion Maps

Here's the mistake we've all been making:

We've been charting the what. But not the why.

We've mapped symptoms, checkups, scripts, refills.

But we haven't mapped:

- The loneliness of 3 a.m.
- The guilt of being a financial burden.
- The quiet shame of forgetting.
- The defiance of googling alternatives.
- The joy of walking up a flight of stairs without stopping—and wishing someone noticed.

Wearables change that.

They listen to what patients don't say.

They see the dips, the pauses, the spikes.

They turn behavior into biography.

The Brand Manager as Biographer

Let me offer a radical thought:

The most successful pharma brands of the future won't be the ones with the sharpest messaging.

They'll be the ones that read between the beats.

Remember that subtle environmental cues can trigger seismic shifts in behavior.

What if the real journey trigger isn't a DTC ad—but a drop in HRV before a panic episode?

What if brand interactions weren't scheduled—but sensed?

What if, instead of pushing a CTA ("Talk to your doctor"), the brand waited—just a beat—until your wearable noticed your breathing shallow during your afternoon commute, then suggested a calm reminder?

This isn't marketing.

This is presence.

Touchpoints, Reimagined

Traditionally, we marked interactions by location:

- Doctor's office
- Pharmacy counter
- Website visit
- CRM email

But wearables let us mark them by state:

- When the patient feels most anxious
- When their sleep has declined for 4 nights
- When stress spikes after work
- When movement stops altogether

Now, the journey isn't driven by clinical milestones.

It's driven by physiological insight.

The Journey Never Paused—We Just didn't see it

Here's what we missed in our old models:

The journey doesn't pause between appointments.

It pulses—constantly.

Every missed step.

Every elevated bpm.

Every restless night.

Every choice not to refill.

Wearables don't just fill the gaps.

They reveal that there were never gaps at all.

Only blind spots.

The Brand as Companion, Not Commander

In the old world, a brand shouted from the hilltop:

"Take your meds. Trust us."

In the new world, the brand sits beside you—silently noticing.

Waiting for the right moment.

Not to sell.

But to say:

"I saw what you're going through. Let's talk."

And That Changes Everything

Suddenly, the brand isn't a company.

It's a character in the story.

A guide. A witness. A prompt.

And the patient?

Not a number. Not a segment.

But a human being with a pulse, a pattern, a narrative.

Which, of course, they always were.

We just needed to listen.

How Wearables Insert Pharma Brands into the Lived Body Experience

When Brands Begin to Breathe with You

How Wearables Put Pharma Inside the Body's Story

In the early 20th century, to reach a consumer, one went to the newspapers.

In the 1950s, you tried their living room—via television.

By the 1990s, you reached into their pockets—thanks to the rise of personal devices.

But now?

Now the most powerful connection point is something far more intimate.

You don't just reach the consumer.

You become part of their body's rhythm.

Welcome to the era where brands don't interrupt your life.

They inhabit it.

The Wrist Knows Before the Mind Does

Consider Maya.

She's 43, juggling two kids, a demanding biotech job, and an autoimmune condition. On paper, she's a textbook case: educated, insured, adherent—pharma's dream demographic.

But Maya isn't on paper.

She's real.

Which means she forgets.

Skips doses.

Sleeps poorly.

Feels guilt.

And Maya wears a sleek band on her wrist.

Every time her sleep dips, her heart rate shifts, or her step count falls for three days straight, the device notices.

One Tuesday morning, her watch buzzes gently:

"We noticed a change. If you've missed your med, it might help to take it now."

It doesn't shout.

It doesn't scold.

It whispers at the right moment, as if the brand had slipped into her nervous system—not to command, but to care.

From the Outside In

Traditional pharma marketing stood outside the body, pointing in:

"Here's what's wrong."

"Here's what might help."

"Here's what to ask your doctor."

But wearables change the angle.

Now, the brand can observe from the inside out:

- Your movement slows.
- Your breathing grows shallow.
- Your sleep fractures.
- Your voice hesitates.

The brand sees not your symptoms, but your signals—physiological breadcrumbs leading back to behavior, emotion, and biology.

That moment of insight?

That's where real trust is built.

The Pill that Feels You Back

Let's imagine for a moment: What if your medicine didn't just treat you—but understood you?

This isn't science fiction.

This is happening.

Think of Abilify MyCite—a digital antipsychotic pill embedded with a sensor that communicates once it's swallowed. It doesn't just go down the hatch. It checks in.

Your body becomes a conversation.

Suddenly, the brand isn't a poster in your doctor's office.

It's a presence in your physiology—tracking, syncing, reassuring.

It's as if the pharmaceutical brand is no longer a company…

…but a quiet second heartbeat.

Brands as Co-regulators of Health

Behavioral psychologists call it co-regulation—the way two people in a relationship unconsciously synchronize breathing, heart rate, mood.

In wearables, brands now play a role in co-regulating your health state:

- Nudging you toward rest when stress peaks.
- Reinforcing action when your willpower dips.
- Noticing when your fatigue may be the first sign of flare-up.

They move from campaign to companionship.

And when the data is right—timely, gentle, earned—this companionship doesn't feel like surveillance.

It feels like support.

The Brand Beneath the Skin

We don't usually think of brands as bodily.

They live in slogans, colors, and logos.

Not in limbs, lungs, or skin.

But wearables—especially smart patches, biosensors, and even ingestibles—blur that boundary.

They give the brand a pulse.

Now, the brand feels your arrhythmia.

The brand knows when your cortisol spikes.

The brand responds when your sleep falters.

Suddenly, pharma isn't just in your medicine cabinet.

It's in your recovery.

In your breath.

In your decisions at 2 a.m.

From Exposure to Embodiment

The greatest challenge in marketing has always been attention.

How to capture it.

How to hold it.

How to convert it.

But wearables aren't about attention.

They're about integration.

Pharma brands move from messaging to embodiment.

They don't have to shout to be noticed.

They're already there—in the rhythm of your day, in the cadence of your sleep, in the vibration that gently says: we noticed you, and we care.

And that Changes Everything

Once, brand interaction was counted in seconds—clicks, impressions, video views.

Now, it's measured in microsignals per hour.

In shared rhythms.

In quiet knowing.

In moments where the brand doesn't just tell a story—

it joins the body's own narrative.

And that?

That's not just marketing.

That's presence.

PART V: ETHICS, PRIVACY, AND THE HUMAN BODY AS A DATA POINT

Part V

Ethics, Privacy, and the Human Body as a Data Point

The Whispering Body: When Your Skin Starts Telling Secrets

In 1965, a Soviet spy named Oleg Penkovsky was caught because he sweated too much.

He was being tailed, unknowingly, by KGB operatives in Moscow. At first, they had no proof—no bug, no note, no phone call. But something gave him away: his perspiration.

It wasn't just the dampness on his shirt. It was the pattern—sudden spikes in his skin's electrical conductivity during specific meetings and walks. The state had learned to listen not to his words, but to his nervous system.

That was sixty years ago.

Today, your wearable can do the same.

Except it doesn't need a shadowy state agency to interpret it. The data is already in the cloud collected, stored, sometimes encrypted, sometimes not.

And it's not a spy who's interested.

It's your insurer. Your employer. Your pharma partner.

Yourself.

Your Body, the Broadcast

There's a moment when your smartwatch senses an arrhythmia and automatically notifies your physician.

It saves your life.

There's another moment when that same data is sold to a third-party analytics firm trying to predict your productivity at work.

You never knew.

Both moments stem from the same source: your body's signals.

Once passive, these signals are now proactive narrators—relaying what you eat, how you sleep, when you falter, and when you rise. They whisper truths before you even know them.

And if you think that sounds dramatic, it is.

Because when the body becomes a broadcast station, the question is no longer what can we hear?

The question is: who's listening—and why?

The Trade we didn't know we made

In 2018, a fitness app that visualized jogging routes inadvertently revealed the location of U.S. military bases overseas. Not because of hacking. Not because of espionage.

Because soldiers—like the rest of us—just wanted to track their runs.

When we say "data is the new oil," we often overlook what that phrase truly means.

Oil, once spilled, can't be unspilled.

Data, once shared, can't be unshared.

Especially when it's not just demographic or behavioral, but biological.

When the Brand becomes the Bystander

Pharma marketers didn't sign up for this moral maze.

They wanted insight, relevance, personalization.

But what happens when your campaign knows someone is slipping into a depressive episode before their therapist does?

Or when an oncology wearable detects early signs of relapse, and the algorithm prioritizes optimizing engagement over notification?

Who decides what to do with the knowing?

The brand?

The patient?

The regulator?

Or the invisible logic of machine learning, optimizing outcomes without explaining itself?

The Ethics of Empathy or Exploitation?

There's a razor-thin line between care and control.

A wearable can nudge a patient toward healthier behavior.

Or it can punish them—adjusting premiums, limiting coverage, triggering compliance emails based on a heart rate anomaly.

The same device.

The same data.

Different intentions.

The Intimacy Paradox

We are at the edge of a paradox:

To truly help someone, you must know them intimately.

But to know someone intimately, you must walk the line of consent, dignity, and trust.

Wearables have placed pharma brands closer to patients than ever before.

So close, in fact, that your product might know when she's pregnant before she does.

So close, that your brand is breathing in rhythm with his anxiety.

So close, that your marketing team may see the body's decline before the body feels it.

And the question isn't: Can we market with that knowledge?

It's: Should we?

The Human Body as Data Point: Awe and Alarm

This is not the surveillance state.

This is the surveillance self—voluntarily connected, eagerly quantified, blissfully unaware of the edge we're dancing on.

We are entering an era where:

- The heartbeat is a metric.
- The breath is a notification.
- The sweat, like Penkovsky's, is a signature.

The body doesn't lie.

But the systems interpreting it? They can.

And so, the most important chapter in the wearable revolution may not be technological.

It may be ethical.

Because the next frontier in pharma isn't innovation.

It's integrity.

Chapter 15

The Surveillance Body

When your Skin Starts Talking, and Someone else Listens

In 1956, a psychologist named Solomon Asch ran an experiment that changed how we understand conformity. A group of young men was shown lines on a card—simple lines, obvious differences—and asked which was the longest. The answer was clear. But when actors planted in the group chose the wrong line, real participants often followed along.

They didn't trust their own eyes.

Now imagine a future where you don't even get to see the lines.

Your wearable device has already decided which one is right.

Your doctor agrees—because the device flagged it.

Your insurer adjusts your premium—because the device saw something.

And you?

You're just the body the data came from.

From Feedback to Surveillance

The line between feedback and surveillance is a fine one. It begins with a buzz on your wrist telling you to move. It ends with a system silently calculating your risk profile based on how often you don't.

The promise of wearables was empowerment.

However, somewhere along the way, optimization gave way to observation.

You are still you—breathing, living, thinking. But now you are also a data stream—pulsing, pinging, performing. Tracked in milliseconds. Judged by algorithms. Predicted before you decide.

You are the watched.

And sometimes, you don't even know who's watching.

Your Data has a Life of its Own

Consider this: A woman in her early 30s downloads a period tracker app. A few weeks later, she buys a connected thermometer. Then she straps on a smartwatch that logs sleep and heart rate variability. She doesn't connect the dots, but her data does.

Somewhere in a data marketplace, a predictive engine flags her as "likely pregnant."

Not to her.

Not to her doctor.

But to advertisers.

She hasn't taken a test yet.

But her body has already spoken.

And someone else—somewhere—is listening.

The Silent Shift in Pharma

When pharmaceutical brands began exploring wearables, they envisioned enhanced patient engagement.

They didn't imagine patient surveillance.

But as data accumulates, and platforms integrate, and algorithms grow more sophisticated, something else happens: the body stops being a private space.

It becomes a node in the network.

Suddenly, adherence isn't just reported—it's monitored.

Side effects aren't self-declared—they're detected.

Behavior isn't described—it's inferred.

And that's when medicine stops asking: "How are you feeling?"

It starts answering: "We already know."

The Judging Algorithm

Imagine this scene:

A teenager with Type 1 diabetes misses three glucose scans in a week. Her wearable transmits the data. A nudging message appears: "Looks like you're falling behind." It's meant to be helpful.

But then her insurer calls. Her monthly refill is delayed pending "follow-up."

Her doctor receives a non-compliance alert.

Her mother gets an email.

Her trust?

Gone.

What began as caring automation now feels like invisible discipline.

She didn't talk to anyone.

But her body did.

And the system listened—and judged.

The Illusion of Opt-In

We're told this is all voluntary. That wearables are opt-in. But consent in a world of persuasive interfaces, pre-checked boxes, and 18-page data policies is often meaningless.

You agreed.

But did you understand?

You signed.

But were you informed?

Most people say yes to terms they never read—because the alternative is exclusion. No device. No service. No insight. No care.

Consent is the new currency.

But the exchange rate? Heavily skewed.

A New Kind of Patient

We used to think of patients as people with diseases. Then we thought of them as empowered consumers. Now?

- Now, patients are performers in an algorithmic arena—scored, sorted, shaped.
- Your resting heart rate may determine your place in a clinical trial.
- Your mobility data may determine whether your cancer therapy qualifies for coverage.
- Your voice tone could signal the start of a depressive episode—and trigger an alert you didn't ask for.

The Watching that Never Stops

There is a story about a parrot in a London apartment that kept calling out, "Alexa, buy cookies!"—until one day, boxes started arriving at the door.

The system wasn't wrong. The parrot had indeed issued a command.

But it hadn't understood the context.

This is the danger of surveillance disguised as care.

Wearables collect contextless truths: a skipped step, a late dose, an elevated heartbeat.

But they don't know about the lost job, the messy divorce, the existential dread.

The body whispers.

But the meaning still lives in the human.

From Oversight to Insight—Responsibly

Wearables can transform pharma. They already are. But if we don't draw lines—clear, ethical, human-first lines—we risk turning patients into datasets, and brands into biosurveillance agents.

What matters now isn't just what we can know, but what we should never assume.

Because a body is not a barcode.

It's a being.

Wearables: The New Frontier of Consent, Autonomy, and Surveillance Capitalism

The Wristband that Whispered

In 2018, a seven-year-old boy in New York wore a fitness tracker to school. He didn't know it would record his every step. His parents bought it to encourage more outdoor play. But when the boy realized his "activity score" was lower than his friend's, he stopped running at recess. He began jogging in place before going to bed. At seven, he wasn't exercising — he was performing.

We thought wearables would give us agency.

But sometimes, they give us anxiety instead.

Not because they are wrong — but because they are watching.

When Data asks No Permission

Back in the 1990s, a Target statistician named Andrew Pole discovered he could predict if a woman was pregnant based on her purchasing behavior: unscented lotion, vitamins, cotton balls. The company sent congratulatory coupons before the woman even told her family.

Now swap lotion for skin temperature.

Swap vitamins for heart rate variability.

Swap cash registers for 24/7 biometric streams.

What once took a spreadsheet and shopping habits now takes a wristband and an algorithm.

Today's prediction is no longer about what you'll do.

It's about who you are — before you even know it.

And that's where surveillance capitalism begins: not in the data itself, but in how it knows you better than you do.

The Mirage of Autonomy

We assume we are in control because we can unpair, uninstall, and delete.

But ask yourself this: Can you truly say no to the thing that's optimizing your health?

Can a heart patient refuse a patch that alerts EMTs in real-time?

Can a clinical trial participant opt out of passive monitoring and still be enrolled?

Freedom becomes an illusion when opting out feels like opting for worse care.

And autonomy, once sacred in medicine, becomes a negotiation with the machine.

The Slippery Consent

Every wearable comes with a tap-to-accept screen.

You accept. You move on. You assume safety.

But those 7,000 words? They don't protect your body.

They protect the platform.

You said yes — but to what?

To who owns your heart rate?

How long can they store your sweat signature?

To where your nocturnal tossing is stored?

To whether your fertility signal is sold?

Consent becomes ritual, not reassurance.

And the ritual hides a deeper truth: We no longer know who's collecting our selves.

The Monetization of the Body

The great shift of the 21st century wasn't that humans went online.

It was that the body went online.

Your sleep is now an ad inventory.

Your blood pressure is a premium signal.

Your breathing patterns feed risk scores.

And somewhere in the boardroom of a pharma-tech joint venture, a heat map shows a thousand patients skipping their meds, glowing red.

Not because they were asked.

But because they were watched.

The Commodification of Compassion

Ironically, it all began with good intentions.

Early wearables were designed to help track steps, improve fitness, warn of atrial fibrillation (AFib), and detect seizures.

But the problem isn't the device.

It's what happens when care becomes commerce.

A patch on your arm records movement.

That data powers an alert.

That alert trains an algorithm.

That algorithm predicts risk.

That risk is sold to an insurer.

The insurer adjusts your premium.

You're not sick.

You're just… less profitable.

And the patch on your arm is no longer just a guardian.

It's a sensor for capitalism.

The Quiet Rebellion

But there's a twist — a reversal.

For every invasive biometric feed, there's a patient who asks a question.

For every surveillance deal struck between tech and pharma, there's a designer saying, "Let's build with dignity."

For every overreach, there's a pause — and perhaps even a pivot.

Because autonomy doesn't vanish. It retreats. And then it fights.

The Real Revolution

The future of wearables isn't just about how much we can track.

It's about how deeply we choose to respect.

Will we build consent into the fiber of every feature?

Will we give people real choices?

Will we remember that health isn't just data — it's being?

If we don't, then wearables won't liberate.

They'll legislate the body.

And we'll have built a system where caring for people… starts to look an awful lot like controlling them.

Legal Frameworks and GDPR/21st Century Cures Act Balance

The Law Wears a Wristband

The Story of Two Laws

In 2016, a quiet revolution took place in Brussels.

A law — thick with clauses, sub-articles, and definitions — passed through the European Parliament. The General Data Protection Regulation (GDPR) wasn't sexy. It didn't launch on stage like an iPhone. But its power? Unmatched.

Across the Atlantic, four months later, another law was born — the 21st Century Cures Act. Its name sounded like hope. Its mission? Acceleration. Faster drug development. More innovation. More data.

In Europe, the law restricted.

In America, the law unleashed.

They were both written with good intentions.

But they were speaking different dialects of the digital body.

And now? They're colliding — on your wrist.

The Human API

Imagine this: A Parkinson's patient in Germany wears a smartwatch. It tracks tremors, sleep, heart rate variability. The pharma sponsor of a trial — based in Boston — wants access to that data. The patient clicks "accept." But then… what?

GDPR says: "Is the data anonymized? Was consent truly informed? Can it be revoked anytime?"

The Cures Act says: "You have a right to access and share your data with whomever you choose."

What's liberation in one system is liability in another.

And caught in the middle is not just the patient — it's the idea of the patient.

Is she a partner? A platform? Or simply a profile?

The Principle of Purpose

GDPR starts with dignity.

It assumes data is an extension of the self.

You can't process it without reason. You can't repurpose it without permission. You can't hoard it in case it becomes useful later.

The Cures Act, on the other hand, leans into openness. Its philosophy is: "If data saves lives, why would we lock it up?"

The European ideal is protection from harm.

The American instinct is permission to innovate.

Both are right.

And both are incomplete.

Because wearables don't fit into neat legal boxes. They're not just medical or just consumer. They're hybrids. They're cyborgs. And the law — built for clean categories — doesn't know what to do with that.

Who Owns the Heartbeat?

You sleep with a wearable. It detects irregular breathing. The data goes to a cloud. The cloud runs a model. The model flags you as high risk. A health system you've never heard of buys that risk score.

Did you consent?

Under GDPR: probably not.

Under the Cures Act: maybe — if you clicked a box.

The problem isn't who owns the data.

It's what ownership even means in a world where your body emits a constant signal — like a lighthouse, whether you want it to or not.

We used to say "my body, my choice."

Now, it's more like "my data, my dilemma."

The Implied Self

There's a clause in GDPR about the "right to be forgotten." A poetic phrase in a legal document. But how do you forget a biometric fingerprint? A gait signature? A medication ingestion timestamp?

The Cures Act encourages interoperability — fluid movement of data across platforms. But what happens when that very fluidity erodes the borders of selfhood?

A person becomes a prediction.

A deviation becomes a liability.

A health insight becomes a monetized moment.

The Wrist, the Watch, the World

The battle between GDPR and the Cures Act is not about bureaucracy.

It's about what it means to be human in the age of quantified selves.

When your heartbeat is a health metric…

Your sleep pattern is a clinical endpoint…

Your skin temperature is a signal of market opportunity…

…who is protecting you — the person?

The law is trying to catch up.

But while it debates clauses and frameworks, the data flows on.

A Future of Mutuality?

The solution isn't choosing Brussels over Washington or vice versa.

It's imagining a new kind of legal contract:

- One that sees the patient not just as a subject, but as a sovereign signal-bearer.
- One where sharing data is an act of agency, not a Faustian trade.
- One that rewards transparency not just in legalese, but in language people understand.
- One that understands that the right to track should never override the right to be free.

In the end, the law must evolve the same way wearables did — from static doctrine to dynamic responsiveness.

Because when the human body becomes a node on the network… we'll need a legal system that remembers the body came first.

Chapter 16

Whose Data is it Anyway?

The Tangled Question of Ownership in the Age of the Quantified Self

The Pulse Problem

In 1965, a Stanford researcher named Edward Green strapped a crude plastic contraption to his chest. It clicked. Whirred. Measured. And spat out one single number: his heart rate.

Green called it a curiosity.

His colleagues called it "extraneous."

The machine didn't improve his pulse. It simply knew it.

That distinction — between improving and knowing — didn't seem so important back then.

But today, it's everything.

Because in our world of Fitbits and biosensor patches, we are no longer just living.

We are measuring.

And the million-dollar question now isn't what we measure.

It's who owns the measurement.

The Mirror that Watches Back

You slip on your smartwatch. It tracks your sleep. It detects an irregular heartbeat. Sends a vibration at 4:12 a.m. You wake up. Schedule an appointment. Your life, perhaps, is saved.

But behind the scenes, your data — that heartbeat, that arousal pattern, that midnight toss-and-turn — is copied, cached, shared, synced. It trains a model.

That model is sold to a pharmaceutical firm that optimizes drug delivery for atrial fibrillation.

They profit.

The model improves.

The app becomes "smarter."

You?

You get a new version… and a discount code for premium features.

It begs the question: Was that your data to begin with?

The Case of the 4,000 Steps

Let's consider a more everyday story. A pharma brand partners with a wearable company. They notice something unusual. Users who walk at least 4,000 steps by noon are 22% more likely to refill their prescriptions on time.

It's a golden behavioral trigger.

So they act: push a notification around 11 a.m. encouraging "a quick walk before lunch." It's subtle. Helpful. "Human-centered," the UX team says.

But the insight came from your footfalls.

Your lunchtime rhythm.

Your body's private choreography.

Again: Whose data is it, anyway?

The Illusion of Consent

Terms and Conditions are the new social contract. You scroll. You tap "Agree." Somewhere in the 47th clause lies this line:

"We may share anonymized data with third-party partners for product improvement purposes."

But what is "anonymized" when your gait is as unique as your fingerprint?

What is "sharing" when you never really owned it in the first place?

We think we're saying yes to an app.

We're actually saying yes to an ecosystem.

And here's the twist: even if you delete your data, the insights it trained — the models, the trends, the personalized nudges — don't disappear.

You can walk away.

But your data-shadow stays behind.

The New Oil... or the New Oxygen?

The metaphor is familiar now. "Data is the new oil." But perhaps it's not oil at all. Oil can be owned. Bought. Sold.

Wearable data? It's more like oxygen.

- It surrounds us.
- Moves through us.
- Invisible until someone builds a device that can read it.
- And suddenly… It's currency.

In this new economy, you don't trade your body.

You trade the patterns of your body.

Your morning jog becomes an algorithm.

Your blood oxygen level becomes a KPI.

Your wrist is a report card.

The Myth of the Individual

In the old world, property was a simple thing. If it was in your house, it was yours. If it came from your body, it was yours.

But wearable data blurs this.

Because yes, it comes from you.

But it only becomes valuable when aggregated, compared, and analyzed.

Your stress spikes mean little…

Until they're studied alongside a million others.

Patterns emerge. Predictions follow. Products evolve.

So is it still yours?

Or is it… ours?

Ownership used to mean control.

Now, it might mean co-authorship.

You're not just the subject of your data.

You're a co-creator of its meaning.

The Road Ahead: Toward Data Mutuality

So, how do we move forward?

The answer lies not in ownership, but in mutuality.

- Not "Who owns the data?"
- But "Who benefits from the data?"

Imagine a world where:

- A Parkinson's patient receives compensation for the tremor data powering a pharmaceutical dashboard.
- A diabetic teen co-designs the algorithm that predicts their insulin needs.
- Patients become partners, not just producers.

This isn't a dream. It's a design decision.

And every wearable on every wrist is a vote — for what kind of future we want.

In the End

The question "Whose data is it anyway?" may seem rhetorical.

But in the era of connected health, it's urgent.

Because data is no longer a byproduct. It's the product.

And the sooner we design systems that reflect that truth — the sooner we move from compliance to trust, from tracking to reciprocity — the better our chances of building a world where technology doesn't just watch the body…

…it works with it.

Data Ownership, Interoperability Battles, and the Looming Presence of Tech Giants (Apple, Google, Amazon) in Health

The Lords of the Cloud: What happens when Silicon Valley Meets the bloodstream?

The Doctor Will See You Now—On an iPhone

In 2020, Dr. Stephanie Jenkins had a patient walk in—not with a folder of lab reports, but with a sleek smartwatch.

"It buzzed at 2 a.m.," he said. "My heart rhythm was off."

He held up his wrist like a badge of technological citizenship.

He didn't want a second opinion.

He wanted confirmation.

The ECG hadn't come from a hospital.

It had come from Apple.

When Health becomes a Platform

Once upon a time, your medical record sat in a steel cabinet behind your doctor's desk.

Now? It sits in the cloud, flanked by your calendar, your playlists, your shopping lists—and every query you've ever whispered to Alexa.

We've quietly shifted from patients to data subjects.

From medical history to data history.

And while pharma companies struggle with pilot programs and dashboards, the tech giants—Apple, Google, Amazon—are building ecosystems.

They don't want to treat the disease.

They want to own the infrastructure of wellness.

The Interoperability Wars

At a hospital in Ohio, a physician can view a patient's blood pressure, weight, and even their medication history—but not the sleep data from their wearable device or the food logs from their phone.

Why?

Because Apple doesn't share with Google.

Google doesn't share with Amazon.

And Amazon... well, Amazon is building its own version of healthcare entirely.

The problem isn't the data.

The problem is who gets to talk to whom.

- Your blood sugar lives on one app.
- Your prescription on another.
- Your insurance data in a third system entirely.

Each one speaks a different language: FHIR, HL7, Apple HealthKit, Google Fit, and Epic's MyChart.

It's as if you're trying to narrate your health in four different dialects... and no one has the Rosetta Stone.

The Data Gatekeepers

Apple positions itself as a champion of privacy.

Your health data stays on your device, encrypted, under biometric lock and key.

Google buys Fitbit—and suddenly has access to the step counts, sleep quality, heart rates of over 100 million users.

Amazon launches Amazon Halo, a wearable that listens to your tone of voice and rates your emotional state.

A company known for selling books now interprets how stressed you sound at breakfast.

They say it's for your benefit.

They say it's empowering.

But ask yourself: Who holds the keys to your digital physiology?

Pharma: A Guest in its Own House

Here's the irony.

Pharma companies have spent decades decoding molecules.

Designing therapies. Running billion-dollar trials.

But when it comes to owning the patient interface, they're often outmaneuvered.

Why?

Because they don't make the devices.

They don't control the platforms.

And they've never mastered the user experience.

Apple doesn't need to run a trial.

It already has millions of users, streaming real-time data voluntarily.

Each iPhone is a walking clinical trial—and Apple doesn't even have to sponsor it.

The Battle for the Biostream

The next war isn't for your medical chart.

It's for your micro-metrics:

- Your heart rate variability after a stressful Zoom call.
- Your REM sleep patterns after a new medication.
- Your cortisol spikes after an argument.

These are not footnotes in a doctor's visit.

They are the frontlines of health data.

And tech giants are setting up camp.

Ownership in a Time of Ubiquity

Let's return to a seemingly simple question: Who owns your health data?

Legally, in many jurisdictions, you do.

But functionally?

- If Apple controls the ecosystem, and can revoke access…
- If Amazon stores it on AWS servers you never see…
- If Google uses it to train predictive models you'll never read…

…is it really yours?

You may own the object, but not the insight.

A Thought Experiment

Imagine this:

You wear a device.

It knows, before you do, that you're slipping into depression.

It alerts a health assistant.

Your medication is adjusted.

You avoid a downward spiral.

Now imagine this same insight is used—without your knowledge—to adjust your insurance premium.

Or deny you coverage.

Or nudge you toward certain behaviors.

Helpful?

Manipulative?

The answer depends not on the data—but on who holds the remote control.

What Happens Next?

We are entering an era where the most valuable asset in healthcare is not a molecule, but a moment—captured by a wearable, interpreted by an algorithm, and sold as a service.

The pharma companies still speak of patients.

The tech giants speak of users.

And in that semantic difference lies the future of medicine.

Case Study: Apple's ResearchKit and HealthKit

Friend or Foe?

A Phone That Became a Lab

On a rainy morning in March 2015, Apple did something quietly revolutionary.

It didn't announce a new iPhone.

It didn't unveil a sleeker MacBook.

It launched a platform—ResearchKit—that turned millions of iPhones into miniature clinical trial sites.

Within weeks, researchers at Stanford had enrolled over 11,000 participants in a heart study.

By comparison, traditional trials often take a year to recruit a few hundred.

All it took? A swipe, a tap, and a consenting thumbprint.

Apple had found a new frontier—not in technology, but in trust.

From Personal Device to Public Health Engine

To understand Apple's move, we need to understand a paradox:

In a world overflowing with healthcare institutions, people often trust consumer tech brands more than their doctors.

The white coat once carried authority.

Now it's the glowing Apple logo that says, "We've got you."

With HealthKit, Apple has centralized every possible biometric, including steps, heart rate, sleep, reproductive health, and even mindfulness minutes.

And with ResearchKit, it gave researchers access to this stream—with user permission, of course.

It was, on paper, a dream scenario:

Researchers could finally break free of the four walls of the clinic.

They could reach patients where they lived, moved, and breathed.

Friend: The Democratizer of Research

Consider a man named Sam in rural Iowa.

Sam has Parkinson's.

For years, he's never been able to travel the 200 miles to the nearest research hospital.

But with Apple's mPower app, part of ResearchKit, Sam can record his voice, test his motor function, and tap through cognitive exercises—all from his living room.

Researchers, in turn, receive real-time, high-volume, longitudinal data.

This isn't science fiction.

It's citizen science, supercharged by UX design.

The beauty of Apple's system is its subtlety.

It captures health in its natural habitat—not under fluorescent lights, but under the sky, between grocery runs, during sleep, after arguments.

It doesn't just ask how healthy you are.

It watches how health happens.

Foe: The Keeper of the Gates

But here's where the story turns.

While ResearchKit is open source, HealthKit—the system that collects, stores, and shares health data—is proprietary.

You can build on it.

But Apple decides the rules.

Imagine a pharmaceutical company wants to study the sleep patterns of hypertensive patients using wearables.

If those patients use iPhones, their data lives in HealthKit.

But can the pharma company access it directly?

No. Not unless the user consents—and even then, Apple mediates the flow.

Apple isn't just the device anymore.

It's the border control.

This isn't inherently malicious.

Apple has built its brand on privacy, and for good reason. In an era of data breaches and algorithmic exploitation, users need a shield.

But in shielding users, Apple also shields the data—and thus controls the terms of engagement.

The Apple Paradox

Let's return to our central question:

Is Apple a friend or foe to healthcare innovation?

The answer lies in the in-between.

Apple is the friend who brought equity to research, modernized patient consent, and enabled passive, real-time health monitoring at scale.

But it is also the gatekeeper who decides which apps can access sensors, who sets the limits of integration, and whose ecosystem is increasingly hard to exit once entered.

Pharma companies, clinical researchers, and digital health startups now face a dilemma:

- Do they build with Apple, and accept its walled garden?
- Or do they stay independent—and risk being left behind?

A Thought Experiment

Let's imagine a future scenario.

A new AI-based therapeutic app can predict manic episodes in bipolar patients, using speech pattern changes and sleep cycles.

It works best on iPhones.

It uses the HealthKit database.

It's ready for rollout.

But Apple, concerned about mental health liabilities, rejects it from the App Store.

Now ask yourself:

Who's making the call—the clinician or the platform?

The shift is subtle but seismic.

Control over tools has morphed into control over treatment pathways.

The Larger Implication

Historically, medical knowledge was held by doctors.

Then it moved to institutions.

Now, it's increasingly held by tech platforms—not in textbooks, but in algorithms and APIs.

ResearchKit and HealthKit represent the double-edged sword of this transition.

They empower.

They centralize.

They democratize.

They monopolize.

All at once.

So, Friend or Foe?

The better question might be:

"Who sets the terms of friendship?"

In Apple's world, data is encrypted, platforms are polished, and users are empowered as long as they stay within the Apple ecosystem.

To some, that's protection.

To others, it's parental oversight with corporate teeth.

In the end, Apple isn't the hero or the villain of this story.

It's the referee.

And in healthcare's next great game, it's writing the rulebook, one update at a time.

Chapter 17

The Empathy Algorithm

The Nurse who Knew Too Much

In the fall of 2003, at a mid-sized hospital in Minneapolis, there was a nurse named Linda who could tell, just by looking at her patients, when something was wrong—before the monitors beeped, before the charts changed, before the labs came back.

Not just when a fever would spike, but when a depression was deepening, or when a patient wasn't saying something vital.

Her colleagues called it instinct.

Her supervisor called it experience.

Linda called it "being there long enough to listen."

Today, we call it something else:

Pattern recognition.

The very same thing that Linda did with her eyes, ears, and gut…

…algorithms are now trying to do with data.

When Machines Learn to Listen

But here's the twist.

What if you could train a machine to do what Linda did?

Not just track heart rate variability or glucose levels, but detect emotional shifts, stress patterns, frustration, or even hope?

That's not science fiction.

That's the empathy algorithm.

It's not about artificial intelligence replacing empathy.

It's about engineering it—finding the physiological signatures of human emotion, and building models that can anticipate needs before they are spoken.

It sounds cold.

But it starts with something warm: the human body.

The Sweat that Spoke Volumes

In 2017, MIT researcher and wearable tech pioneer Rosalind Picard told a story.

She had built a wristband to monitor electrical activity on the skin—EDA, or electrodermal activity. She gave one to a boy with autism, just for data collection.

One night, his chart showed something strange:

A huge spike in EDA—the kind seen in extreme stress or seizures.

But here's the odd part:

It didn't appear on the wrist that moved—it was on the non-dominant, motionless wrist.

Why? Because the algorithm wasn't misreading.

The boy wasn't showing it outwardly, but he was in distress.

He was silently seizing.

The wearable knew—before anyone else did.

And that's when Picard realized: this wasn't just tracking.

This was listening.

The Algorithm with Feelings

Fast-forward to today.

Wearables aren't just counting steps.

They're reading the unsaid.

- A dip in HRV (heart rate variability) might mean fatigue—or emotional withdrawal.
- A change in galvanic skin response could indicate anxiety—even before the patient reports it.
- Patterns in tone, texting frequency, or movement rhythms might predict a relapse in depression.

These aren't just biomarkers.

They're empathy signals—read not by people, but by code.

That's what researchers at companies like Empatica, BioBeats, and Affectiva are trying to decode.

They're not asking machines to feel.

They're asking them to notice.

When Pharma Listens Differently

Imagine a pharma brand for bipolar disorder.

Instead of waiting for symptoms to return, it pairs its medication with a wearable device that tracks subtle shifts, including sleep patterns, speech tempo, and skin conductivity.

One morning, the wearable senses a change in circadian rhythm, a slight elevation in resting heart rate, and delayed response patterns.

It nudges the patient with a soft message:

"Would you like to speak to someone today?"

It alerts the clinician—not with panic, but with early signs.

This is empathy, not in tone, but in timing.

The machine doesn't care.

But it knows when we do.

From Compliance to Companionship

Traditional pharma asked:

Did the patient take the pill?

Empathetic pharma asks:

Why did they stop?

Was it fatigue? Side effects? Social pressure? Or quiet despair?

The empathy algorithm doesn't judge.

It simply connects the dots: between a dropped workout, a muted phone, and a disrupted sleep cycle.

It understands that non-compliance is rarely irrational.

It's human.

And if brands want to be trusted partners in care, they must do what Linda did back in that hospital:

Watch. Listen. Understand.

The Turing Test of Care

Alan Turing once asked:

Can a machine convince you it's human?

Today's question is subtler:

Can a machine convince you it cares?

In a world where pharma often struggles to gain emotional proximity to patients, empathy algorithms offer a bridge.

Not to replace human connection, but to scale it.

Not to monitor patients, but to support them silently.

Like a good friend who checks in without being asked.

Like a nurse who knows, just by looking.

A Final Thought

The real magic of the empathy algorithm isn't in its math.

It's in its motive.

It doesn't calculate care.

It predicts suffering—and reaches out before the silence deepens.

That's not artificial.

That's amplified humanity.

And perhaps the next great breakthrough in pharma marketing isn't a new molecule or mechanism…

…but an algorithm that simply says:

"I noticed. And I'm here."

Can Biosignal-Triggered Marketing be Ethical?

The Pulse of a Moment

In 2021, a woman in Chicago received a notification on her smartwatch moments after her heart rate spiked. She wasn't exercising. She wasn't running. She was simply scrolling through photos of her late father.

The alert wasn't from her cardiologist.

It was from a mental wellness app she'd downloaded six months earlier and forgotten.

"Feeling tense? Take a breath with us.-"

It wasn't wrong.

It just… knew.

This wasn't a coincidence.

It was biosignal-triggered marketing—a silent revolution where your body becomes the trigger, and a message becomes the response.

But here's the question:

If a company markets to your heartbeat, is it still your decision?

The Skin Knows First

There's something poetic about it:

Your skin tingles.

Your sweat glands activate.

Your heart stutters.

And somewhere, in the cloud, a system decides you need help.

Or a discount.

Or a dose.

Or a prompt.

A prompt that seems eerily timely.

"Looks like stress is up—want to refill your sleep aid?"

"HRV is down—need support for your anxiety?"

"Skipped three meals? Consider our nutrition plan."

It's not guessing.

It's reading you.

But here's the dilemma:

When does reading become manipulation?

The Attention Economy Moves Inward

Historically, marketers chased eyeballs, then clicks, and now micro-moments. But wearables changed the game.

Now, marketing taps into something far more intimate:

The involuntary signals of your autonomic nervous system.

No surveys. No focus groups. Just sweat, pulse, and sleep.

What was once a whisper of attention becomes a pulse of opportunity.

But that pulse—should it belong to you, or to the brand?

Between Empathy and Exploitation

Let's pause.

- What if biosignal-triggered messaging helps?
- A reminder nudges a patient to take life-saving medication.
- A signal detects impending panic and offers cognitive tools.
- A heartbeat warns of an arrhythmia before a collapse.

That's not marketing.

That's a lifeline.

But what if it shifts?

- You're marketed a supplement every time your cortisol spikes.
- A pharma brand sends content every time your HRV dips.
- Your insurance premium goes up—because you skipped your walk.

Now, the line blurs.

Is it help… or pressure?

Is it support… or surveillance with a sales target?

The Ethics of Timing

In 2012, Target infamously predicted a teenage girl's pregnancy before her father did—using purchase data.

Now imagine Target had access to her sleep cycle, skin temperature, and emotion signals.

That's where biosignal marketing sits today:

On the knife-edge between hyper-personalization and hyper-intrusion.

The message may be kind.

But the moment—chosen by your biology—is not.

Who permitted for grief to become a trigger?

The Consent Illusion

You clicked "Accept" once. Maybe years ago.

You agreed to share heart rate for "health optimization."

But did you realize that included targeted nudges at your most vulnerable points?

Most users don't.

Because the data is invisible.

The consequences are subtle.

And the marketing?

It's wrapped in wellness.

It whispers, not shouts.

But beneath the velvet glove is a powerful hand:

A hand that knows you better than your conscious self.

Hope, Not Hype

Let's be fair.

Biosignal-triggered marketing can be ethical.

But it needs more than innovation.

It needs intention.

Not: "How can we convert this heart rate dip into a sale?"

But: "How can we ensure this nudge respects autonomy, dignity, and consent?"

It requires:

- Transparent data practices.
- True opt-in, not buried T&Cs.
- Firewalls between health data and commercial algorithms.
- Boundaries for when not to market at all.

It requires marketers with moral compasses, not just conversion goals.

Because when a brand enters the bloodstream—metaphorically or literally—it should come with a code of ethics, not just a creative brief.

The Final Beat

So: Can biosignal-triggered marketing be ethical?

Yes.

But only if it feels like empathy, not exploitation.

Only if it protects silence, not just seizes opportunity.

Only if it asks, rather than assumes.

In a world where machines read bodies faster than minds do, ethical restraint becomes a new form of innovation.

Because your heartbeat isn't just data.

It's you.

And when a brand listens to that heartbeat…

It must first learn how to care.

Emotional AI and Pharma's Responsibility to Use it Wisely

The Algorithm that Felt Too Much

In the spring of 2024, a teenager in Bangalore opened her wellness app after a long, sleepless night. The app greeted her, not with a cheery motivational quote, but with something altogether different:

"We sense elevated distress. Would you like to talk to someone?"

She hadn't entered any data. She hadn't filled out a mood tracker.

She had only worn her smart ring.

The app wasn't guessing. It had noticed a change in her heart rate variability, her galvanic skin response, and her nocturnal movement patterns.

In short, her emotional baseline had shifted.

This was emotional AI.

And it knew—before she did.

The Empathy Equation

Emotional AI doesn't read minds. But it comes disturbingly close.

It infers mood from micro-patterns.

It senses agitation from eye blinks, sadness from vocal pitch, anxiety from skin conductivity.

It learns from thousands of biological breadcrumbs to predict:

You are sad.

You are distracted.

You are losing hope.

Now imagine that AI is not part of a school wellness app…

But a pharma brand's engagement platform.

You're depressed.

Your biosignals show it.

A nudge arrives:

"Our new fast-acting antidepressant could help. Tap to explore."

Helpful? Perhaps.

But here's the catch:

The AI knew you were vulnerable before you did.

Responsibility in the Age of Emotionally Aware Algorithms

The pharmaceutical industry has always walked a moral tightrope:

Balancing science with sales, hope with profit, innovation with ethics.

But emotional AI is different.

It isn't about targeting demographics.

It's about targeting the nervous system.

A brand manager can now design campaigns that react to a patient's despair in real time.

Push notifications sent when sadness peaks.

Messages personalized to match emotional states.

Even drug titration suggestions, tailored to subconscious distress.

It's powerful.

It's precise.

It's potentially dangerous.

Because empathy without accountability becomes exploitation.

The Cambridge Analytica of Feelings

We've seen this before.

A data company promises to "understand you better."

To "deliver only relevant experiences."

To "personalize your journey."

Until the data gets weaponized.

Until knowing someone's emotional state becomes a way to influence, nudge, manipulate—without consent.

Emotional AI in pharma must not go the same way.

It can't just be another layer of personalization.

It must be a sacred trust.

Because what's more intimate than your genome?

Your emotional pattern.

And when a company holds that—

They don't just hold data.

They hold you.

Empathy at Scale: Can Machines Truly Care?

The technologists behind emotional AI say their systems are "empathetic."

They detect distress.

They modulate tone.

They adapt interfaces to emotional needs.

But can an algorithm really care?

No.

It can simulate concern.

It can respond to triggers.

But it cannot hold space.

Only humans can do that.

So when pharma uses emotional AI, it must never pretend the machine is the caregiver.

The tech is the tool.

The human responsibility remains.

To know when not to nudge.

To know when sadness is not a sales opportunity.

To build firewalls between marketing and emotional telemetry.

The Asimov Rule for Emotional Data

Perhaps it's time to borrow from science fiction.

Isaac Asimov once imagined a world where robots followed three unbreakable laws.

Maybe emotional AI in pharma needs its own:

1. Do no emotional harm.
2. Preserve emotional autonomy.
3. Enable healing, never manipulation.

Simple.

Human.

Necessary.

Because the more emotion we extract from biosignals, the more care we must encode into their use.

The Soul in the Stream

We've come a long way from branded pens and doctor's office brochures.

Now, pharma companies can whisper into a person's life—not through slogans, but through their sorrow.

That is not just marketing.

That is medicine masquerading as a message.

And if they choose to use emotional AI, they must ask themselves:

"Are we soothing a wound… or selling into it?"

Because every biosignal is a heartbeat, and every heartbeat is a life.

Not a lead.

PART VI: LOOKING FORWARD – THE NEXT PHASE OF THE WEARABLE EDGE

Part VI

Looking Forward – The Next Phase of the Wearable Edge

The Future, Strapped to Your Wrist

In 1973, a young engineer at the Hamilton Watch Company helped create the first digital wristwatch.

It cost more than a used car.

It told the time—nothing more.

It was considered a miracle.

Fifty years later, that same wrist real estate tracks your blood oxygen, alerts you before a panic attack, warns of atrial fibrillation, and whispers to your phone, your physician, and—perhaps without you knowing it—your pharmaceutical provider.

What changed?

Not the wrist.

Not the need for time.

But the idea of what time could tell us.

The future of wearables isn't about shrinking chips or adding more sensors.

It's about redefining the very notion of intervention, identity, and intimacy in health.

From Reactive to Predictive. From Predictive to Preventive. From Preventive to... Prescriptive?

Until recently, the pharmaceutical industry existed in a reactive paradigm.

A disease emerged. A symptom appeared.

A treatment followed.

Then wearables arrived—and suddenly, we weren't reacting anymore.

We were predicting.

We were preventing.

And now, in the next phase of the wearable edge, we are beginning to prescribe experiences.

A wearable doesn't just track your steps.

It trains your behavior.

It anticipates your needs.

It guides your decisions before you even know they're decisions.

This is no longer device + data.

It is intelligence + intimacy.

And that shift changes everything.

Health is No Longer a Place. It's a Pattern

Hospitals used to be where health happened.

Then came clinics.

Then home diagnostics.

Now?

Now, health is ambient.

It follows you.

It listens when you breathe.

It learns from how you sleep.

It lives in your biometric trail—collected passively, constantly, and computationally.

In this world, the patient is not a passive recipient of care.

They are a data stream.

A pattern of probabilities.

A biological narrative in motion.

And for pharma, the challenge is no longer: "How do we market our molecule?"

It's: "How do we become part of that story—ethically, empathetically, and enduringly?"

From Devices to Ecosystems to Digital Twins

Tomorrow's wearables will not be devices.

They will be ecosystems.

Networks of connected sensors that speak to each other—and to your future self.

Already, researchers are building digital twins—replicas of your biological systems in silico, trained on your own wearable data.

Want to know how you'll respond to a new hypertension drug?

Your twin will try it first.

Want to test a lifestyle change, a dietary tweak, a shift in your sleep cycle?

Let your avatar simulate it in real-time.

The line between modeling and medicine is blurring.

And that's not science fiction.

That's the new clinical trial—personalized, continuous, predictive.

The Last Mile: Trust

But even as the algorithms evolve and the dashboards multiply, one question remains unchanged:

Do people trust this?

Trust is not built in the lab.

It's not encoded in firmware.

It's earned at the moment of need.

When a wearable says, "Call your doctor now,"—will we believe it?

When a pharma brand nudges, "Your symptoms suggest you may benefit from X,"—will we welcome it?

The final phase of the wearable edge is not technological.

It is emotional.

Relational.

Human.

Because at the edge of all this innovation is not a chip.

It is a person.

Breathing. Wondering. Deciding.

Welcome to the Threshold

So this is not a conclusion.

It is an invitation—to reimagine what pharma marketing can be in a world where health doesn't just happen in hospitals, but in habits.

In heartbeats.

In hunches from data we haven't yet learned how to feel.

The next phase of the wearable edge is already here.

It just hasn't been evenly understood, regulated, or wielded—yet.

And perhaps that's the real challenge for every brand manager, technologist, ethicist, and storyteller in the pharmaceutical industry:

Not to make wearables smarter…

But to make the people who use them feel seen, not just scanned.

Chapter 18

The Rise of Wearable Ecosystems

In 2007, a man named James Park clipped a small device onto his waistband and went for a walk. The device counted his steps.

That's it.

No voice assistant. No GPS. No Bluetooth. Just steps.

That device would become the first Fitbit.

And that walk? It would become the first steps toward a revolution—not just in wearables, but in how we live inside technology.

Today, you don't just wear a tracker.

You live inside an ecosystem.

Your steps talk to your heart rate, which talks to your sleep cycles, which whisper to your phone, which syncs to your doctor, who may one day prescribe a drug that's adjusted in real-time based on how your body responds to it—all without you lifting a finger.

How did we get here?

It didn't Start with Devices. It Started with Decisions

The genius of wearables wasn't in their hardware.

It was in their habit loop.

Wearables didn't just collect data.

They changed behavior—quietly, imperceptibly, one vibration at a time.

You took more steps.

You slept a little better.

You felt seen—not by a person, but by an interface.

And slowly, the device on your wrist became the most intimate mirror of your life.

Not because it told you what you were doing, but because it made you ask: Why am I doing this at all?

Now multiply that across sleep rings, glucose monitors, menstrual cycle trackers, pulse oximeters, digital pills, and smart inhalers.

Suddenly, we're no longer talking about gadgets.

We're talking about an operating system for the human body.

From Standalone to Symphonic

A single wearable was once enough.

But then something curious happened.

We began to want our devices to talk to each other.

A smart patch that tracks inflammation needs to know what a CGM is sensing.

A sleep tracker needs context from your physical activity.

An arrhythmia alert means more when correlated with stress markers and HRV.

And so, the ecosystem emerged.

Apple didn't just sell you a Watch—they gave you HealthKit.

Google didn't just acquire Fitbit—they positioned it inside a universe of predictive search, AI, and biometric feedback.

Amazon's Halo didn't ask what you were doing—it asked how you sounded while doing it.

Each brand wasn't offering a product.

They were inviting you into a walled garden of wellness.

Where your breath was a datapoint.

Where your voice was a vital sign.

Where your sweat held secrets.

Pharma's Wake-Up Call

Pharmaceutical companies watched this from the outside for a while—curious, cautious.

Their model was molecule-first.

Wearables? That was Silicon Valley's playground.

But then came the data.

Data that could show how drugs were actually working—not just in trials, but in real life.

Data that could predict who would adhere, who would abandon, who might decline before they reported a symptom.

And suddenly, pharma began to see wearables not as gadgets, but as extensions of therapy.

Not just adherence tools, but engagement platforms.

What once lived in spreadsheets and sales rep pitches now lived on the body.

A pill was no longer enough.

A platform was needed.

And so, we saw partnerships bloom:

Dexcom with Verily.

Pfizer with Fitbit.

Sanofi with Happify Health.

Novartis with Propeller.

Takeda with Biofourmis.

These weren't deals.

They were ecosystem entries.

The New Competitive Advantage: Integration

In the age of ecosystems, it's no longer about who has the best sensor.

It's about who can orchestrate the most meaningful connections.

Can your smart patch talk to my oncology platform?

Can your sleep data inform my digital therapeutic?

Can your real-time ECG be interpreted through my AI, under FDA approval, across three continents?

The winners in this new world aren't the ones with the most features.

They're the ones who create fluidity—where the user doesn't feel the system, but becomes empowered by it.

That's why ecosystems matter.

They turn discrete moments into continuous meaning.

But Be Careful what You Connect

Because when everything connects—everything listens.

When your body becomes a network, it also becomes vulnerable.

To overreach.

To surveillance.

To opaque data trades and unseen algorithms.

The same systems that deliver hyper-personalized care can also lead to hyper-targeted persuasion.

The question isn't whether ecosystems will dominate pharma.

They already are.

The question is:

Will these ecosystems liberate the patient?

Or will they just create a more intimate form of dependency?

The Future isn't Wearable, it's Inhabitable

In the end, the wearable revolution was never really about what we wore.

It was about what we became.

We didn't just strap on a device.

We stepped into a feedback loop that never sleeps.

We moved from passive patients to active participants.

From data collected to data felt.

From tools that tracked our pulse… to systems that shaped our path.

And that ecosystem?

It's still evolving.

Still expanding.

Still waiting for those bold enough—not just to connect the dots—but to ask: What kind of world are we building, one heartbeat at a time?

Interoperability between Devices, Drugs, Dashboards, and Doctors

The Hidden Conversation: How Interoperability Redefines Modern Medicine?

In the spring of 1971, a young man in Boston walked into Massachusetts General Hospital wearing an unusual contraption strapped across his chest. It wasn't a stethoscope or a blood pressure cuff. It was a custom-built biofeedback harness connected to a computer the size of a filing cabinet. The man? Steve Mann, later dubbed the father of wearable computing. The contraption? A prototype of the first "wearable computer"—a system that could track physiological changes in real time.

But there was one problem.

No one knew what to do with the data.

The Babel Problem in Healthcare

Imagine walking into a room where everyone is speaking a different language: one speaks French, another speaks Mandarin, a third uses Morse code, and someone else just points at pictures. Now imagine all of them trying to explain how your body is responding to a medication… while your heart rate is fluctuating.

That's what the early wearable-tech-medical landscape looked like.

Smartwatches recorded your pulse.

Patches measured hydration.

Pills dissolved with microchips.

Doctors scribbled notes in EMRs.

And pharmaceutical reps tracked outcomes… on spreadsheets.

All of it was happening. None of it was talking.

Interoperability wasn't a feature.

It was the missing conversation.

A Body Without a Brain

It's easy to be dazzled by a sleek wearable that tracks your sleep, distance walked, and even your stress levels. But without interoperability, it's like listening to a violinist warming up—beautiful, but isolated.

Now imagine an orchestra.

Your wearable senses atrial fibrillation.

The dashboard alerts your cardiologist.

The cardiologist sees that you haven't refilled your beta-blocker prescription.

The pharmacy dispatches a reminder.

And your digital coach texts: "Skip the evening coffee. Let's focus on hydration today."

This is not just care.

This is orchestrated care.

But for that to happen, every element—device, drug, dashboard, and doctor—must speak a shared language.

That shared language is interoperability.

The Magic of the Right Hand Talking to the Left

In the late 1990s, a strange phenomenon occurred in aviation.

Two pilots nearly crashed a plane—not because of engine failure or bad weather—but because their autopilot systems weren't "interoperable." One was guiding altitude; the other, speed. Each thought the other was in control. No alarms. No errors. Just silence. Near-fatal silence.

Healthcare's version of that?

- A patient wearing a glucose monitor synced to their phone, but not to their insulin pump.
- A cancer patient logging pain on a smart patch—only to have the oncologist never see it.
- A clinical trial with perfect biometric adherence, but with data siloed in four portals, each with a different login.

Technology without translation is as good as no technology at all.

The Power of Connected Meaning

The magic isn't in the device.

It's in the connections.

When your wearable speaks to your electronic health record, when your pharma-issued smart inhaler transmits data to your provider dashboard, when AI models adjust treatment algorithms on the fly based on that incoming stream—it's no longer "remote monitoring."

It's augmented medicine.

And that's the kind of medicine that can learn from each breath, each missed pill, each restless night—and adjust the symphony accordingly.

Interoperability is not just a Technical Challenge, it's a Philosophical One

You see, interoperability isn't only about APIs and data schemas.

It's about trust.

It asks:

- Who owns the data?
- Who gets to see it?
- Who gets to act on it?

When your heart rate drops during a workout, should your Apple Watch notify your doctor? Your insurance company? Your employer?

These are not technical questions.

These are human questions.

And they lie at the heart of how we build connected systems that serve people instead of just tracking them.

The Four I's of Interoperability

1. **Insight:** Devices must not just record—they must understand what they're seeing.
2. **Integration:** Drugs, sensors, apps, and care platforms must seamlessly integrate with each other, much like instruments in a jazz band.

3. **Interpretation:** Data must be humanized. The doctor shouldn't get raw pulses; she should get patterns.
4. **Impact:** All this orchestration must lead to one thing: better outcomes.

Otherwise, what's the point?

The Future is a Conversation, Not a Command

Wearables have evolved.

Drugs have evolved.

Even dashboards have evolved.

Now, it's time for medicine to listen to itself.

When the body speaks—through electrical impulses, skin temperature, cortisol fluctuations, or tremor patterns—we must ensure that every part of the healthcare system is listening.

That means devices that talk to dashboards.

Dashboards that talk to doctors.

Doctors who are guided by algorithms.

Algorithms refined by real-world behavior.

And all of it looping back—to you.

Because in the end, you are the common language.

And interoperability?

That's just the healthcare system finally learning how to listen in harmony.

Open Platforms Like Open mHealth and Apple's Ecosystem Approach

The Garden and the Bazaar: How Open Platforms are Redrawing the Map of Digital Health?

In the 1980s, a young software engineer named Richard Stallman stood on the threshold of a locked lab door. The lab, once a communal space where coders shared ideas freely, had adopted a proprietary system. The door was now secured by password. The source code—once open—was now a secret.

For Stallman, it wasn't just about code.

It was a matter of ethics.

That moment sparked the birth of the open source movement—a belief that technology, to be useful, must be interoperable, transparent, and shareable.

Decades later, in a world of biosensors and smartwatches, the healthcare industry finds itself at that same metaphorical door.

And the question being asked is:

Should we build gardens or bazaars?

A New Kind of Architecture

In one corner stands Apple.

Elegant. Walled. Impeccably curated.

An ecosystem so seamlessly integrated that it feels like magic. Your Apple Watch talks to your iPhone, which nudges your Health app, which feeds ResearchKit and CareKit and HealthKit—each layer an invisible bridge between your body and your data.

In the other corner is Open mHealth.

Open-source. Modular. Collaborative.

It offers a Lego kit for digital health—components that anyone can build on, remix, or extend. A place where a small startup in Nairobi can integrate sleep data from Garmin with clinical trial endpoints and build an app overnight. No NDAs. No app store restrictions. Just raw potential.

One system is a cathedral.

The other, a bazaar.

And the story of digital health hinges on the tension between the two.

The Cathedral: Apple's Symphony

Apple's approach to health is like a Bach fugue—each note in sync, each product finely tuned. There's brilliance in the coherence.

With HealthKit, Apple created a health data hub that consolidated information from countless devices into a single, encrypted, user-controlled vault.

Then came ResearchKit, which transformed clinical trials by turning iPhones into diagnostic tools. Overnight, studies that once took years to recruit could sign up thousands with a swipe and a consent form.

But it came with strings.

Access was conditional.

Data was boxed within the Apple environment.

To be part of the Apple health ecosystem, you had to play by Apple's rules. And those rules, while elegant, often meant friction for researchers and limits for innovation.

It's like owning a Stradivarius violin—exquisite, but you can only play it at the Apple Concert Hall.

The Bazaar: Open mHealth's Rebellion

Then there's Open mHealth—a nonprofit initiative co-founded by Deborah Estrin and David Haddad, with a simple but radical idea: Make health data interoperable. Period.

They didn't build an app. They built a standard.

Want to compare sleep data from Fitbit and Withings? Use Open mHealth schemas.

Want to pull glucose data into an oncology dashboard? There's a module for that.

They created building blocks, not walls. The kind of system that thrives not because it's controlled, but because it's shared.

Open mHealth's world is messy, diverse, and sometimes slower. But it's also scalable. And it gives birth to innovations Apple might never dream of.

Because when you throw open the gates to creativity, unexpected things walk in.

Why it Matters to Pharma?

This isn't just a debate about operating systems.

It's about the future of medicine.

Imagine a pharma brand designing a wearable-powered clinical trial. Do they go with Apple's toolkit—polished, beautiful, restrictive? Or do they build on Open mHealth—flexible, messy, but owned?

If they choose Apple, they get ease and engagement—a ready-made audience with 100 million wrists.

If they choose Open mHealth, they get portability and partnership—a chance to reach the unreached and build truly global health solutions.

It's not one vs. the other.

It's a question of intent.

Are we designing for control?

Or for collaboration?

Lessons from Linux and Lego

Think of the world of wearable data as analogous to two revolutions:

- Linux, which quietly powers 90% of the world's servers, was built on open collaboration.
- Lego, which exploded in popularity when it opened its design platform to fans, now credits its community with its biggest hits.

Likewise, Open mHealth may never have Apple's polish. But it has something arguably more powerful: permissionless innovation.

And that is the seedbed of the next wearable health revolution.

The Future is a Hybrid

Innovation doesn't always come from the center. It often comes from the edges.

From the small lab, the indie coder, the underfunded clinician with a big idea.

That's the promise of Open mHealth.

But elegance has its place too. Apple's coherence accelerates trust, engagement, adoption.

The future? It's not the garden or the bazaar.

It's a public square—where the best ideas of both worlds meet.

Where Apple's polish integrates with open standards.

Where open platforms adopt Apple's UX discipline.

And where patients and brand managers alike don't have to choose between usability and freedom.

In this future, wearables become infrastructure—and health becomes interoperable by design.

Chapter 19

Pharma + AI + IoT = The Intelligent Health Loop

In 1901, a young Hungarian physician named Ignaz Semmelweis noticed something peculiar. Women who delivered babies in the hospital's midwife ward had dramatically lower mortality rates than those in the doctor's ward. The only difference? The doctors—often coming straight from autopsies—didn't wash their hands.

Semmelweis proposed a radical idea: handwashing could save lives.

He was mocked. Dismissed. Laughed out of medicine.

He died in an asylum.

Today, it's hard to imagine healthcare without the antiseptic ritual of clean hands.

And yet, a century later, we're once again standing on the edge of a paradigm shift just as profound.

This time, the revolution isn't in soap and water.

It's in data.

And it's powered by the convergence of pharma, AI, and the Internet of Things (IoT).

It's a story of sensors embedded in skin, algorithms whispering patterns from noise, and pharma marketers who no longer wait for illness—but anticipate it.

Welcome to the Intelligent Health Loop.

The Loop Begins with a Beat

In a clinic in rural Iowa, a woman wears a discreet adhesive patch just below her collarbone. It tracks her heart rate variability, sleep quality, movement, skin temperature, and respiratory patterns—24/7.

She's not sick.

She's participating in a post-market surveillance program for a new immunotherapy.

Her wearable isn't just recording. It's learning.

At midnight, her patch detects a drop in HRV and a subtle elevation in body temperature. An AI model, trained on thousands of similar patients, flags it—not as an emergency—but as an early signal.

A nudging text: "Hi Jane, how are you feeling today? Consider checking in with your care team."

The loop is engaged.

The brand has not sold a drug.

It has delivered trust.

From Dumb Pills to Smart Loops

For decades, pharma operated on a linear model:

Discover a molecule.

Test it.

Package it.

Sell it.

Repeat.

The patient journey was episodic.

Adherence was a black box.

Feedback loops were slow, expensive, and often came too late.

But now, with IoT sensors capturing biometric data, AI analyzing the real-time flux, and pharma embracing digital ecosystems, the model is no longer linear.

It's circular.

Just like a smartwatch that closes your "rings," the Intelligent Health Loop constantly collects, interprets, adjusts, and responds—not after symptoms appear, but before.

What Happens when a Drug Listens?

Consider Novartis.

In a 2022 trial for heart failure, they didn't just measure hospitalizations. They partnered with wearable device firms to track breathlessness, daily step count, and nocturnal coughing—feeding data into an AI engine that learned each patient's baseline.

When that baseline shifted—subtly, almost imperceptibly—AI flagged risk.

Pharmacists intervened early. Dosages adjusted.

Hospital visits dropped by 12%.

It was no longer a pill with a label.

It was a living feedback system.

The Marketer becomes the Behavior Architect

But the health loop doesn't end in the lab.

It extends into the everyday behaviors that drive outcomes.

Pharma marketers, once focused on brochures and booth banners, now study biosignals. They ask: When is this patient most likely to feel anxious? When are they most motivated?

Using machine learning, they sequence content—delivering a mindfulness reminder after poor sleep, a medication nudge after elevated BP, or an empathetic message when stress levels rise.

This isn't just marketing.

It's micro-coaching.

And it's as intimate as a whisper.

When Tech Giants Come Knocking

Of course, the intelligent loop has its titans.

Google's Verily builds health dashboards from sensor clouds.

Amazon's Halo band listens for tone and stress.

Apple's ResearchKit feeds anonymized data into hundreds of studies.

They bring scale, design, and frictionless interfaces.

Pharma brings biology, regulatory acumen, and molecular innovation.

Together, they create something entirely new:

A continuously adaptive health platform, where medicine isn't prescribed—it converges with behavior.

The Feedback Effect

In 1956, psychologist Albert Bandura showed that feedback shapes behavior more than punishment or reward alone.

In 2025, AI confirms it.

A study of over 10,000 asthma patients wearing connected inhalers (like those from Propeller Health) found that real-time alerts and pattern-based coaching increased adherence by 58% and reduced ER visits by nearly half.

The magic wasn't in the device.

It was in the loop:

Data → Insight → Action → Adjustment → Data.

It's no longer "a product."

It's an experience.

And it lives in the space between the dose and the decision.

From Reactive to Reflective Pharma

The intelligent health loop doesn't just make pharma smarter.

It makes it more reflective.

It demands ethical conversations:

- Who owns the loop?
- Can AI overrule doctors?
- Should biosignals trigger behavioral nudges without consent?

The loop raises questions not just of technology, but of intent.

And that, perhaps, is the greatest shift:

Pharma, once defined by molecules, is being redefined by mindfulness—of context, of timing, of individual experience.

The Semmelweis Moment

Like Semmelweis, today's innovators are telling us to look—closer, earlier, deeper.

That health is not what happens in hospitals,but in the micro-decisions, micro-signals, and micro-moments that wearables now capture.

That a pill is only half the story, unless it plugs into a loop that listens, learns, and adapts.

This is not science fiction.

It's science, looped.

And for the first time in pharma history, the product isn't the drug.

It's the relationship.

Real-Time Feedback, Predictive Diagnostics, and Digital Twins

The Mirror that Anticipates

In 1968, a Harvard psychology professor named B.F. Skinner made an observation that would quietly revolutionize how we learn. He called it the principle of "immediate reinforcement." Simply put: behavior that receives instant feedback is far more likely to change.

Give a rat a pellet after a lever press—behavior forms.

Give a human a gold star for spelling a word right—learning accelerates.

Wait too long, and the loop fades.

Fast-forward half a century. The feedback loop hasn't just shrunk.

It's now instantaneous, intelligent, and invisible.

It lives in a wristband.

Or a smart patch.

Or a pill.

It doesn't just respond.

It predicts.

And sometimes—almost eerily—it knows you better than you do.

The Feedback Loop that Breathes

Imagine waking up groggy after a poor night's sleep. Your smartwatch vibrates, not to punish you, but to adapt your goals. Fewer steps today. A hydration reminder. A prompt to breathe.

This isn't a nudge. It's a conversation.

Real-time feedback has moved from passive tracking to active coaching.

It interprets, adjusts, nudges.

It does what Skinner dreamed of—only now, with AI as the teacher and your own body as the syllabus.

From Mirrors to Crystal Balls: Predictive Diagnostics

In the 1800s, doctors diagnosed by touch, by smell, by the color of sputum. They were artists—intuitive, often brilliant, sometimes wrong.

Today, diagnosis is moving away from hunches toward predictive models—based not on symptoms, but on sub-threshold signals that would have been invisible to the naked eye.

Consider this:

A sudden drop in heart rate variability.

A mild elevation in skin temp.

A shift in gait pattern so subtle it escapes human notice.

To a physician, it's noise.

To an AI, it's a signature.

In one pilot, wearable data predicted heart failure exacerbations 6 days before clinical symptoms.

In another, continuous glucose monitors flagged insulin resistance weeks before HbA1c changes.

Diagnosis is no longer a moment.

It's a stream.

And in that stream, the future ripples into view.

The Phantom Patient: Enter the Digital Twin

In 2002, NASA began simulating entire spacecraft systems as virtual replicas—a practice they called "digital twinning." Every bolt, every wire, mirrored in software to predict failures before they happened.

Now, that same concept is being applied not to rockets—but to people.

A digital twin is your physiological mirror:

Your heart rate. Your breathing. Your medication response curves. Your genome.

A living, learning model of you, continuously updated, tested, and simulated.

Pharma companies like Dassault Systèmes and Siemens Healthineers are building these models to simulate how a specific drug might affect your liver enzyme, your inflammatory markers, your side effect risk.

What used to take a trial can now be modeled in milliseconds.

It's as if you have a shadow self, trying the medication first.

If it fails, you never take it.

If it works, it's already personalized.

This isn't medicine.

It's forecasting.

It's weather reports for your biology.

The Implications: Knowing Too Soon?

But with prediction comes paradox.

What happens when your twin sees an Alzheimer's signature before you feel foggy?

Or when your real-time dashboard shows you a cardiac risk score on your 45th birthday?

Do you change?

Do you panic?

Do you trust it?

Real-time feedback and predictive diagnostics demand something more than data science.

They demand philosophy.

Because in knowing ourselves so deeply, we may be forced to confront a more vulnerable truth:

Foreknowledge without agency is fear.

Which is why the role of pharma—and marketers—is no longer just to inform.

It's to contextualize.

To guide.

To empathize.

Skinner would Smile

Behavioral science told us long ago that feedback shapes behavior.

But what it didn't predict was this:

That our own bodies would become the sensors.

That our diseases would whisper before they shout.

That a twin made of code would stand beside us, quietly rehearsing our future.

It's not science fiction.

It's the quiet revolution happening on our wrists, under our skin, and in the cloud.

And it doesn't just tell us where we've been.

It tells us where we're going.

Before we even get there.

Case: Philips HealthSuite and IBM Watson Health Partnerships

The Second Opinion Machine: Philips, Watson, and the New Clinician

In the 1960s, when Dutch engineer Bob Haans was working in a dimly lit lab in Eindhoven, the idea was simple: make healthcare more visual. Philips was perfecting the first ultrasound systems, allowing doctors to see into the body—noninvasively, in real time.

Half a century later, Philips isn't just giving doctors better eyes.

It's giving them a second mind.

Not a human one.

A synthetic one.

One that doesn't blink, forget, or tire.

One that listens to millions of data points, and whispers: "Here's what matters."

And sometimes, it even knows before the doctor does.

The Birth of HealthSuite: From Devices to Decisions

Philips had always been about hardware. Monitors. Scanners. Ventilators.

But by 2014, something shifted.

Their machines were collecting oceans of data.

Heartbeats. Breathing rates. Sleep cycles. Medication logs.

But no one was listening to it.

HealthSuite was born not to create more data—but to make it speak.

Built as a cloud-based platform, it unified hospitals, devices, and homes into one seamless loop.

If a patient's heart rate dropped at 3:12 a.m., HealthSuite knew.

If oxygen saturation dipped, it could nudge the nurse.

And if a diabetic's glucose started trending dangerously high, HealthSuite could call.

It wasn't just healthcare anymore.

It was health awareness.

Enter Watson: The Doctor who Read Everything

Meanwhile, across the Atlantic, IBM had its own ambition.

It had built a computer named after its founder, Watson, who once said, "Think."

Watson had beat Jeopardy champions on TV.

But now, IBM wanted it to beat cancer.

Not with drugs.

With words.

Watson could read 200 million pages of medical literature in seconds.

It could compare patient genomes with case reports.

It could remember every clinical trial ever run on glioblastoma.

In 2017, IBM and Philips joined forces.

The idea?

Let Philips 'devices monitor life in real time…

…and let Watson make sense of it.

The New Stethoscope: An AI Symphony

Imagine this:

A cancer patient, recently diagnosed. The oncologist has two hours before the consultation.

The EMR is 80 pages. The patient has four comorbidities. Three potential treatment pathways.

The doctor logs into a portal.

Watson has already reviewed the chart, flagged clinical trial matches, and highlighted two published papers the physician hadn't seen.

HealthSuite, meanwhile, has been quietly tracking the patient's vitals, showing that her oxygen saturation is dipping faster on one drug.

Together, they form a third colleague.

Not a replacement.

An augmentation.

It's as if the stethoscope now speaks back, saying:

"Doctor, here's what I see. Doctor, here's what you may have missed."

When a Machine Hums Alongside a Human

This isn't about replacing intuition.

It's about relieving overload.

Studies show that physicians must read 29 hours a day to stay current with new research.

The average ICU patient generates over a million data points per day.

Humans were never meant to keep up.

But with AI as a companion—quiet, ever-learning—the playing field shifts.

Philips 'partnership with the Dana-Farber Cancer Institute used Watson to assist in complex oncology decisions.

Elsewhere, HealthSuite integrated predictive algorithms for COPD patients to prevent emergency hospitalizations.

Doctors began catching subtle signals sooner.

Patients felt more seen, more heard.

Not because humans tried harder.

But because the machines helped them listen better.

The Ghost in the Machine: What Happens Next?

But with this brilliance comes a quiet question.

If Watson knows better…

If HealthSuite intervenes earlier…

Who takes responsibility when it fails?

When a machine suggests—does the human always agree?

When a platform nudges behavior—whose ethics apply?

Philips and IBM weren't just designing technology.

They were, perhaps unknowingly, redesigning trust in medicine.

And in this brave new world of wearables, cloud brains, and second opinions from machines, maybe the question isn't whether the AI gets it right.

Maybe the question is:

Can we, as humans, learn to collaborate with something that never sleeps?

Chapter 20

Future-Proofing Pharma with Wearables

In 1999, a little-known pharmacist in Tokyo noticed something peculiar. His teenage asthma patients were returning for refills less frequently, not because they were cured, but because they were simply forgetting their medication. So he did something radical: he attached a small, blinking light to their inhalers. The light didn't dispense anything. It just blinked. Quietly. Persistently. Like a reminder from a caring friend.

Six months later, adherence went up by 22%.

Now, imagine that blinking light got smarter. It began to sense pollen in the air, read respiratory rates, detect subtle changes in breathing during sleep, and buzzed you—gently—before your lungs even knew they were about to tighten.

That's the world pharma is stepping into. And wearables aren't accessories anymore.

They're infrastructure.

The Cold Start Problem

Pharma, for all its might and science, has always had a curious problem.

It's late to its own party.

It invents drugs—breakthroughs even—but enters markets with the urgency of a librarian, not a futurist. Trials run slow. Regulations move slower. And by the time marketing teams adapt to the next channel, patients have already moved on to the one after that.

Wearables offer something pharma has never really had:

Proactive presence.

Not after symptoms begin. Not after a drug is launched.

But before. Before the cough, before the blood sugar spike, before the missed dose.

That's not just treatment.

That's insurance against irrelevance.

From Molecules to Moments

The pharmaceutical industry was built around molecules.

What if its future was built around moments?

The moment someone's heart skips a beat on a stairwell.

The moment their sleep quality dips four nights in a row.

The moment their smartwatch detects microtremors hours before their Parkinson's meds are due.

In that moment, the brand that shows up—relevant, timely, reassuring—wins.

Wearables turn pharma into a real-time actor in a previously silent drama.

Not just a company that sells pills. But one that knows the person. Understands the rhythm. Anticipates the need.

That's not just good marketing. That's future-proofing.

The Trust Dividend

When Abbott launched the FreeStyle Libre—a wearable glucose sensor—it didn't just win on tech.

It won on transparency.

No more finger pricks. No more secrecy. Patients could see their data. Act on it. Share it.

Abbott stopped being a company that made devices. It became a partner in behavior change.

This is the hidden promise of wearables for pharma:

Not better devices. Not better data.

But better trust.

And in a world where public perception of pharma swings like a metronome—from vaccine saviors to pricing villains—trust isn't just a nice-to-have.

It's currency.

The 3Rs of Future-Proofing: Real-time, Responsive, Responsible

Let's imagine pharma like a jazz musician.

- Real-time: Sensing the rhythm of the patient's life through continuous streams of biosignals.
- Responsive: Improvising not just treatments but nudges, alerts, encouragements, even silence—when needed.
- Responsible: Knowing when to play and when to step back. When to store data, and when to let it go. When to serve the science, and when to serve the soul.

Because the future of pharma isn't just digital.

It's ethical.

It's relational.

It's wearable.

The Dilemma of the Invisible Brand

Here's the irony.

The more effective wearables become, the more invisible the pharma brand risks becoming.

If your watch tells you to walk, your ring nudges hydration, your patch adjusts your dose—who gets the credit?

The Drug? The Device? The Data?

The future-proofed pharma brand won't compete for visibility.

It will compete for utility.

The brand becomes ambient. Like good lighting or warm water—subtle, essential, unforgettable once experienced.

That requires a mindset shift:

From logos on packaging to algorithms in lives.

From awareness campaigns to integration into bio-behavioral rhythms.

A Glimpse Forward

In 2030, a teenage girl with epilepsy wears a thin, nearly invisible sensor under her skin.

It tracks neuro-signals and sends micro-doses of medication via a transdermal patch the moment her data predicts a spike in seizure probability.

She never visits the ER.

She doesn't even think about it.

It's just her life. Lived, quietly, safely.

Her pharma brand? It never once appears in a TV ad.

But it's with her, in every sense.

And So—The Final Insight

Wearables may have started as fitness fads.

But for pharma, they are not gadgets. They are guardians.

They offer the chance to pivot from a transactional industry to a transformational force.

From pills that sit on a shelf, to partnerships that move with you.

From chasing prescriptions, to shaping behaviors.

From curing disease, to nurturing health.

To future-proof is not to predict the future.

It is to become the kind of company the future can't do without.

And in that quiet hum on your wrist, in that pulse-synced vibration that reminds you to breathe, in that passive sensor that knew you were slipping—long before you did—there lies not just technology…

…but a new kind of medicine.

How to Prepare Your Brand, Your Team, Your Technology Stack?

In the early 2000s, Blockbuster had everything going for it: dominance, data, distribution. It had the brand. It had the team. It had the technology—at least by the standards of the time. And yet, one quiet upstart, Netflix, rewrote the story.

Why?

Because Netflix understood one thing: Technology doesn't just support a brand. It changes its identity.

The real lesson wasn't about streaming versus DVDs.

It was about how companies prepare themselves for the change they don't see coming.

Wearables, in pharma, are that unseen change. Not because we don't know they exist. But because most teams are preparing for them the way Blockbuster prepared for digital—with nostalgia and reluctance.

So what does it really mean to prepare your brand, your team, your tech stack—for the wearable edge?

It means starting from the inside out.

1. **Your Brand: From Message to Mission**

   Ask any pharma marketer what their brand stands for, and you'll hear words like "efficacy," "compliance," "clinical outcomes."

   Now ask a patient wearing a smart patch what they want: peace of mind, freedom from fear, subtle support, and a feeling that their life—not just their lab values—matters.

   Here's the first shift: Your brand is no longer a message. It's a behavior.

   A wearable-integrated brand must live inside the user's rhythm. It must anticipate rather than declare. It must show up in micro-moments: when the user wakes up, walks, eats, skips a dose, sleeps too little, or breathes too fast.

   Brands must shift from promising outcomes to delivering experiences.

   It's no longer enough to say, "We care."

Your wearable-enabled feedback loop should whisper: We know when to care—and how.

2. **Your Team: From Functions to Fluency**

   In 1970, if you were a brand manager in pharma, you needed to know two things: the product and the prescriber.

   Today? That same brand manager must be a translator.

   Between hardware engineers and health psychologists.

   Between AI scientists and regulatory teams.

   Between patient advocacy voices and pricing strategists.

   And most of all, between the data and the story.

   Preparing your team means developing what psychologists call cognitive flexibility—the ability to switch contexts, perspectives, and disciplines without losing clarity.

   It's no longer about having a digital department.

   It's about being a digitally fluent culture.

   Not everyone needs to code.

   But everyone needs to know what's possible when a wearable speaks, and what happens when no one's listening.

3. **Your Technology Stack: From Stack to Storyline**

   Let's be honest.

   Most pharma tech stacks were built like bunkers: secure, siloed, impenetrable.

   But wearables don't live in bunkers. They live on bodies—messy, real, unpredictable bodies.

   They demand integration, interoperability, and instantaneity.

   And here's the twist: the tech stack of tomorrow isn't just about efficiency. It's about empathy.

   If your CRM doesn't allow real-time syncing of biosensor triggers, it's not just outdated.

   It's insensitive.

   If your analytics dashboard can't translate variability in heart rate into behavioral risk, you're not just behind.

You're blind.

Your technology must evolve from a stack to a storyline—one that follows the patient, adapts to them, and loops back insights in a way your team can act on today.

This means investing not just in software, but in sensor literacy, API openness, data ethics frameworks, and most of all—time to train the humans who will use it.

The Paradox of Preparation

Preparation, we often think, is about control.

But in the age of wearables, it's about humility.

Wearables teach us that the body is always speaking.

The best-prepared brands, teams, and tech stacks are those that learn not to shout over the signal—but to listen, interpret, and adapt.

Preparing for wearables isn't about being the first to launch a patch, a ring, or a pill with a chip.

It's about being the last brand the patient would ever want to let go of.

Because you understood their pulse—not just their prescription.

Because your team could respond—not just report.

Because your system could sense—not just store.

Insight to Take Forward:

"Being ready is no longer about being right. It's about being responsive. And responsiveness, in the wearable age, is the new form of wisdom."

Building Alliances with Startups, Regulators, and Tech Platforms

In 1976, a young, shaggy-haired Steve Jobs walked into a room of seasoned HP engineers and showed them a prototype. It was fragile, untested, and laughably small compared to the hulking mainframes they were used to.

They dismissed him.

He wasn't asking them for money. He was asking them to imagine a world where the underdog and the incumbent didn't have to be enemies.

Fast forward to today's pharmaceutical industry. The question facing executives isn't whether to adopt wearable technology. It's who to adopt it with—and how to trust them.

Because the future of pharma won't be built in a boardroom.

It will be co-architected at the intersections—where regulation, innovation, and ambition collide.

The Startup Dance: Agility Meets Authority

Let's start with startups.

A behavioral scientist might say that startups exhibit what's known as "exploratory bias"—they favor risk, speed, and novelty. In contrast, pharma companies have a well-earned "exploitation bias"—they favor consistency, compliance, and risk management.

One tests. The other verifies.

One says, "Let's try this."

The other says, "Prove it."

And yet, when these biases are harnessed together—when a startup's pulse-sensing patch meets a pharma brand's global trial infrastructure—magic happens.

Take the example of Propeller Health and GSK. What began as an outsider startup tracking asthma inhaler use became a quietly revolutionary alliance. GSK brought the muscle. Propeller brought the edge.

But the key wasn't technology. It was trust.

They shared data, not just dashboards.

They shared failure, not just press releases.

In the wearable age, startups aren't vendors.

They're co-authors of your next clinical chapter.

Regulators: From Gatekeepers to Collaborators

It's easy to caricature regulators as the brakes in the system. But that's like blaming the referee for slowing the game.

In reality, regulators are becoming coaches—guiding the industry toward what matters: safety, efficacy, and ethical clarity.

Consider the FDA's Digital Health Software Precertification Program. Instead of waiting for devices to land on their desk, the FDA is co-creating standards with developers and pharma alike.

This isn't just regulatory evolution.

It's behavioral adaptation—a willingness to learn from wearables rather than merely review them.

Smart pharma companies are learning a counterintuitive lesson: invite regulators earlier, and you go faster.

Build alliances not with lawyers in tow, but with product managers, ethicists, and patients at the table.

Because when regulators feel like stakeholders, they stop saying "no," and start asking "how."

Tech Titans: Platforms or Predators?

And then there are the tech giants.

Apple. Google. Amazon.

They already sit on the wrist. In the pocket. On the nightstand. They have what pharma has always wanted: daily relevance.

But relevance isn't the same as respect.

Pharma knows how to earn trust with 10-year trials. Tech knows how to gain adoption with 10-second UX. Both want health outcomes. But they speak in wildly different dialects.

So, what does a smart alliance look like?

Not just APIs and cloud storage.

But shared governance over data.

Shared goals on patient empowerment.

Shared guardrails around emotional AI.

Take Apple's ResearchKit. It's open-source, user-consented, and built with academic partners. Now imagine a pharma alliance where study recruitment happens via Apple Watch, adverse event flagging via Siri, and real-time dose adjustment via biosignal loops.

In that world, Apple doesn't eat pharma's lunch.

It helps set the table.

But that requires one thing pharma has never been good at: co-branding control.

The Pivot

Remember change doesn't begin with a moment—it begins with a shift in mindset. With reframing the obvious. With looking at the outlier and asking, "What if they're not crazy—but early?"

That's the lesson here.

Startups aren't threats. They're scouts.

Regulators aren't obstacles. They're navigators.

Tech platforms aren't rivals. They're bridges—if we choose to walk them together.

The future of pharma isn't a fortress. It's a village built on interoperability, curiosity, and mutual consent.

And the alliances we form now—with the bold, the cautious, and the code-literate—will determine whether wearables stay a gimmick… or become the heartbeat of a new kind of care.

Chapter 21

Stitching the Signal — A Practical Guide to Integrating Wearables into Your Pharma Marketing Strategy

In the summer of 2014, a small team at Apple sat around a table, arguing—not about design, or software, or hardware—but about the human wrist.

They weren't engineers that day. They were anthropologists of movement.

"Is this really where health lives now?" someone asked.

A few miles away, at Stanford, cardiologists were sketching the ECG waveform on a whiteboard. Across the country, brand strategists at Johnson & Johnson were wondering: could this little square of glass on the wrist detect atrial fibrillation before a cardiologist did?

It wasn't a product launch. It was the beginning of a new relationship between body, brand, and biology.

This chapter is about how to get that relationship right—strategically, ethically, and empathetically.

1. **Start with the Body, Not the Brand**

   Before logos, dashboards, or marketing emails, start here:

   - What physiological or behavioral signal correlates most closely with the pain point your product solves?
   - If you're in diabetes, it's glucose variability, real-time.
   - If you're in oncology, maybe it's fatigue or pain episodes.
   - For depression, perhaps it's activity, sleep, and heart rate variability.
   - In asthma, inhaler usage and ambient air quality matter more than "adherence" alone.

   This isn't data science. It's clinical empathy.

You're not choosing a device. You're choosing a proxy for human suffering—and building trust on top of it.

2. **Matching Tech to Therapeutic Area**

Choosing the right wearable isn't a procurement exercise—it's diagnostic strategy.

Let's break it down:

Therapeutic Area	Core Signals	Ideal Wearable Form Factors	Examples
Diabetes	Blood glucose, HRV	Steps, CGMS (pathces), Smart pens	Dexcom + Lilly
Cardiology	ECG, HRV	Step cadence, Smartwathces, ECG-enabled wearables	Apple Wathc + J&J AFib Study
COPD / Asthma	Inhaler Use, Peak flow motion	Smart Inhalers, Chest Patches	GSK + Propeller
Depression	Sleep, HRV, Movement, Speech	Smartwatches, Smartphone Sensors	Verily + Mental health teams
Oncology	Plain, Fatigue, HRV, Sleep	Wearable biosensors (Empatica)	Takeda + Empatica
Neurodegenrative	Tremor, Gait, Balance	Accelerometer-enabled smartwathces	Roche + Apple

The question isn't "What can this device do?"

It's: "What human experience can it decode?"

3. **Development: Build or Partner?**

Most pharma companies won't design their own devices (nor should they). But they will need to answer:

- Do we license an existing wearable platform?
- Do we co-develop a disease-specific variant?
- Or do we integrate our molecule into an existing hardware/software loop?

Three pathways emerge:

1. White-labeled Integrations: e.g., Your asthma drug + Propeller's smart inhaler platform.
2. Companion Apps + AI Layer: e.g., A sleep optimization AI that nudges antidepressant compliance.
3. Drug-Device Convergence: e.g., Ingestible sensors (Proteus) or insulin-smart pen ecosystems (Lilly + Dexcom).

The most successful partnerships aren't built on technology. They're built on a shared definition of patient value.

4. **Integration: Stitching Signals into Strategy**

Your wearable is not a standalone product. It must be integrated into:

- Your CRM tools (to adjust engagement)
- Your trial design (to inform endpoints)
- Your adherence tracking
- Your real-world evidence gathering

Ask: Where in the patient journey does this data alter decision-making or experience?

For instance:

Touchpoint	Wearable Trigger	Brand Action
Missed a walk (COPD)	Drop in movement + HRV spike	Send a supportive breathing exdrcise video
Fatigue detected (Cancer)	Lower HRV + disturbed sleep	Offer digital check-in or support option
Glucose spike (Diabetes)	CGM alert + Sedentary period	Recommend light movement or water intake

The magic lies in the microintervention.

Wearables make it possible. But strategy makes it meaningful.

5. **Stakeholder Engagement: A Conversation of Trust**

   1. **Healthcare Providers**

      They're overwhelmed. Give them context, not noise.

      What to show:

- Clear, visualized trends (HRV, gait speed, fatigue over time)
- How this data supports better titration, not more alerts
- Regulatory validation and peer-reviewed trials

How to deliver:

- CME-accredited webinars
- Patient case journeys
- EHR-integrated dashboards (pilot first)

HCPs don't need "more innovation."

They need tools that feel clinical, not commercial.

2. **Internal Teams (Brand, Legal, IT, Compliance)**

Build an interdisciplinary squad. Treat the wearable as both:

- A product extension (legal + regulatory)
- A marketing enabler (brand)
- A data asset (IT + analytics)

Checklist for alignment:

- Data privacy frameworks (GDPR, HIPAA, etc.)
- Defined KPIs: engagement uplift? adherence boost? trial cost savings?
- Fail-fast pilot culture: launch → learn → iterate

3. **Patients**

Don't lead with features. Lead with emotional benefits.

Instead of:

"Track your HRV to optimize compliance."

Say:

"Your body tells a story. We're here to help you listen."

Co-design with patients. Pay attention to:

- Device comfort and aesthetics
- Cultural attitudes toward tracking
- Simple language, not scientific jargon
- Transparent consent flows

Trust is your campaign.

4. **Regulators**

   They're not your enemy—they're your allies in clarity.

   - Share early prototypes and data logic models
   - Anticipate concerns: accuracy, intrusion, long-term data use
   - Offer pre-competitive collaborations: industry-wide standards (like Open mHealth)

     A well-prepared regulatory team is your invisible launch partner.

6. **Metrics that Matter**

   Forget vanity metrics. Here's what truly signals success:

Objective	Metric
Improve adherence	% uplift vs. control (real-world or pilot)
Enhance engagement	Response rate to wearable-triggered interventions
Enable better outcomes	Reduction in ER visits, relapses, flare-ups
Increase brand loyaly	Retention, refill, or switch-back behavior
Generate real-world evidence	Validated biomarker correlations + patient-reported outcomes

   But don't stop there.

   Ask: Did we make the patient feel more seen, safer, or stronger?

   That's a strategic KPI, too.

7. **Storytelling in the Sensor Age**

   Data informs. But story transforms.

   As you integrate wearables, remember:

   - Every signal is a scene.
   - Every patient journey is a narrative arc.
   - Every campaign touchpoint is a dialogue.

   Wearables don't just track movement.

   They move brands—when handled with care, curiosity, and conscience.

Stakeholder Communication Plan: Turning Signals into Shared Vision

When a wearable device becomes part of your brand strategy, it's not just technology—it's a message. And every stakeholder hears it differently. This plan ensures they not only hear, but understand, engage, and act.

1. **Patients: Turning Data into Dignity**

   What they care about: Simplicity, control, transparency, and value.

   How to communicate:

   - Tell real-life stories: How a patient used the wearable to predict a crisis before it happened.
   - Use plain, empowering language: "This device listens to your body when you can't."
   - Address fears: data privacy, comfort, and purpose—always.
   - Tools: Explainer videos, onboarding kits, chatbot walkthroughs, patient champions, community forums.

2. **Healthcare Professionals (HCPs): From Devices to Decisions**

   What they care about: Clinical relevance, workflow integration, and peer evidence.

   How to communicate:

   - Lead with evidence: Present peer-reviewed outcomes and clinical validation.
   - Speak in the language of efficiency and outcomes: "This tool reduces time to diagnosis by 27%."
   - Involve KOLs and early adopters as advocates, not just endorsers.
   - Tools: CME webinars, quick-reference dashboards, EHR-integrated tools, clinical use-case briefs.

3. **Caregivers: From Overwhelm to Insight**

   What they care about: Peace of mind, ease of use, and proactive alerts.

   How to communicate:

   - Frame the wearable as a silent partner, not another chore.

- Use empathy-first communication: "This device keeps watch so you can be present."
- Tools: Companion apps, alert systems, FAQ booklets, "Caregivers' Corner" platforms.

4. **Payers and Insurers: From Devices to Dollars**

   What they care about: Outcomes, cost savings, adherence, and ROI.

   How to communicate:

   - Quantify impact: "Wearable monitoring reduced readmissions by 22%."
   - Share real-world evidence and longitudinal adherence data.
   - Position as a value-based care tool, not a gadget.
   - Tools: Health economic models, case studies, reimbursement briefs, pilot programs.

5. **Regulators: From Innovation to Integrity**

   What they care about: Safety, transparency, compliance, and evidence.

   How to communicate:

   - Engage early and often: Share protocols, data architecture, privacy standards.
   - Highlight alignment with FDA/EMA frameworks and 21st Century Cures Act mandates.
   - Tools: Regulatory whitepapers, privacy documentation, continuous auditability systems.

6. **Internal Teams (Medical, Legal, Regulatory, Commercial)**

   What they care about: Clarity, cross-functionality, risk mitigation.

   How to communicate:

   - Create a shared narrative: "Why this wearable? Why now?"
   - Foster internal alignment with workshops, simulations, and strategy maps.
   - Tools: Internal playbooks, AI-assisted briefing decks, co-creation sprints.

7. **Tech Partners and Developers: From Specs to Shared Goals**

   What they care about: API access, uptime, roadmap alignment.

   How to communicate:

   - Build relationships beyond contracts—emphasize purpose fit, not just feature fit.
   - Use bi-directional planning to align innovation timelines.
   - Tools: Co-design frameworks, agile collaboration boards, developer documentation kits.

8. **Investors and Leadership: From Innovation to Impact**

   What they care about: Strategic advantage, differentiation, and future-proofing.

   How to communicate:

   - Link wearable strategy to brand vision, market growth, and competitive moat.
   - Showcase proof-of-concept traction and scalability pathways.
   - Tools: Executive dashboards, market impact forecasts, investor storyboards.

Final Note: Communication as Co-Creation

In the wearable age, communication isn't just delivery—it's design. Pharma brands that win in this space don't just talk at stakeholders—they co-create meaning with them.

Let every signal captured by a device become a message, every insight a story, and every stakeholder an advocate in your connected care revolution.

Conclusion

Always On, Always Human

In 1960, Dr. Paul Zoll—one of the pioneers of cardiac pacing—warned that putting electronics inside the body might cross "a moral boundary." At the time, the idea of living with machines monitoring your heartbeat sounded like science fiction, or worse, science gone too far.

Today, millions of people wake up, glance at their wrists, and know—in a heartbeat—how they slept, how they moved, even how they felt.

What changed?

Not the human body.

Not the need to feel safe, seen, and cared for.

What changed was trust—in data, in design, and in each other.

Wearables didn't become part of our lives because they were inevitable.

They became part of our lives because they made us feel more human.

The Tipping Point of Intimacy

We used to talk about customer touchpoints—emails, brochures, office visits. Now we talk about touchwear—fabric that listens, patches that whisper, implants that negotiate dosage with biology in real time.

And while pharmaceutical marketers once aimed to "capture attention," they now occupy a space so intimate, it would make Don Draper blush: the circadian rhythm. The HRV dip. The skipped beat before anxiety peaks.

What does it mean for a brand to be always on?

It means letting go of campaigns and embracing continuous conversations.

It means replacing interruption with intervention—small, timely nudges based on biosignals rather than demographics.

It means recognizing that every ping, prompt, or pulse-triggered suggestion is not just a message, but a moment of trust—earned or lost.

The Humanity Inside the Data

It's tempting, in an AI-fueled, API-integrated, cloud-synced future, to believe that we're moving away from the messiness of human life.

But look closer.

That wearables detect anxiety doesn't make us less human.

That pharma can pre-empt a migraine or manic episode doesn't make it mechanical.

That behavior can be nudged doesn't mean it's manipulated.

What it means is: we are finally designing care around the rhythms of real life.

One researcher put it best: "We're not just quantifying the body. We're learning how to listen to it."

The irony is:

We thought wearables were about control.

What they offered was connection.

We thought they would distance us—from doctors, from decisions, from discomfort.

Instead, they made us feel—more responsible, more aware, more alive.

The Edge is Not the End

Pharma is standing at a threshold—not of technology, but of ethics, empathy, and intention.

The companies that thrive will not be those with the sleekest sensors or boldest dashboards. They'll be the ones that ask the real question: How do we honor the trust that comes with knowing someone's heartbeat?

That's the wearable edge.

It's not just about data. It's about dignity.

It's not about being first. It's about being felt.

It's not about being always on.

It's about staying always human.

Because in the end, the future of pharma will be worn not on the wrist or chest—but in the space between biology and belonging.

And that future starts now—not with a launch, but with a listening ear.

Where Technology Ends and Humanity Begins

At some point, every generation has stood at the crossroads of invention and identity.

The printing press.

The steam engine.

The microchip.

And now—the biosensor.

Each was greeted with awe and suspicion. Each promised a better future while casting shadows on the present. And each, in its own way, forced us to ask the same question:

Where do we end, and the machine begins?

The Seamless Blur

Walk into a home today and you'll see a child with a glucose sensor on her arm, a grandfather with an implantable loop recorder beneath his chest, a mother whose smartwatch just reminded her to breathe.

Are they machines now?

No more than a man reading by candlelight in Gutenberg's day became one with the press. No more than the typist merged with the typewriter.

The truth is subtler.

When a tool is wielded at arm's length, we call it technology.

When it becomes invisible—when it slips under the skin, syncs with our rhythms, adapts to our moods—something shifts.

It is no longer used.

It is lived.

And in that shift lies the paradox: the more intimate the tech, the more human the questions become.

The Mirror, Not the Mask

Wearables don't change who we are.

They reveal who we've always been—creatures of habit, emotion, cycles, and longing.

They map our anxieties. Track our hope. Alert us to danger. Reward our effort.

They are not armor or artifice.

They are mirrors—held up to the pulse of our being.

And yet, for all their sophistication, they lack one thing.

They do not know why we wake up with fear.

They cannot tell if a racing heart means joy or sorrow.

They cannot feel what it is to be touched, or to forgive, or to remember a scent from childhood.

Only we can do that.

And so, the line becomes clearer.

The Line in the Sand

Technology ends not at the skin, but at the soul.

It can measure rest, but not peace.

It can predict behavior, but not meaning.

It can optimize care, but not offer compassion.

The dashboard may blink with metrics.

The AI may recommend a new dosage.

The wearable may nudge us toward a healthier choice.

But only a human can say, "I understand."

Only a human can decide when enough data is enough.

When rest matters more than resolution.

When presence is better than precision.

The Final Thought

In the end, we wear these devices not to become less human—but to remember how human we are.

The beating heart is not an algorithm.

The body is not a platform.

And life, in all its mess and mystery, cannot be debugged or downloaded.

We are not just quantified selves.

We are storied selves.

Searching. Striving. Surviving.

Still listening for meaning beneath the signal.

So, perhaps the question isn't where technology ends.

It's where humanity begins again—each time we choose to feel, rather than just track; to connect, rather than just compute; to care, rather than just calibrate.

In that choice lies the true future.

Not of devices.

But of us.

The Algorithm Can't Hold Your Hand

Why Pharma Marketing in the Wearable Age Must Stay Human, Story-Driven, and Ethically Grounded

Let's begin not with a wearable—but with a wrist.

More precisely: the wrist of a man named George. Sixty-two. Former smoker. A retired bus driver from Akron, Ohio. He wears a smartwatch prescribed by his healthcare provider. It vibrates every morning at 7:00 a.m., reminding him to take his beta-blocker. It notices when he's restless at night. It flags his heart rate when he climbs stairs.

One Thursday afternoon, the device flashes a new message:

"Your heart rate variability suggests elevated stress. Try a mindfulness exercise."

George looks at the message. He's not stressed. Not today. Not in any way the watch could know. He's grieving—his wife of 34 years passed away last month.

And the watch?

It doesn't know that.

It can't know that.

And in that single, silent moment lies the case for human-centered, story-driven, ethically grounded pharma marketing in the wearable age.

The Problem of Perfect Predictions

The allure of wearables is intoxicating. Real-time data. Continuous feedback. Micro-personalization. Imagine a world where a pharma brand could send George not just a reminder for his meds, but a message tailored to his stress pattern, his sleep quality, his daily step count.

The marketing strategist dreams: "What if we could always send the right message at the right moment?"

But here's the twist: being right isn't the same as being human.

A machine can know that George's cortisol is high.

But only a story can tell why.

That distinction—between knowing and understanding, between targeting and empathizing—isn't just philosophical. It's practical. Because marketing that forgets the story forgets the person.

And people don't buy treatments. They buy hope. They buy relief. They buy connection.

They buy a story in which they still have control.

From Biofeedback to Belief Systems

Consider what happens when pharma marketing becomes purely data-driven. The brand speaks in numbers:

- 15% risk reduction.
- 24-hour efficacy window.
- 3x improvement in adherence with wearable reminders.

It's rational. Precise. Impressive.

But it doesn't stir the soul.

Now consider a different message:

"I used to be terrified of flare-ups. Then I saw how this helped me sleep through the night. It gave me back my mornings."

That's not data.

That's testimony.

That's narrative.

In a world where wearables quantify everything, stories still humanize everything.

The Ethical Compass in a Hyperconnected World

With great data comes great responsibility.

When your watch knows your mood before your spouse does…

When your wearable detects early signs of depression before you do…

When a brand can send you a personalized nudge at the exact moment you're vulnerable…

Then we're no longer just talking about marketing.

We're talking about power.

And power—untethered from ethics—leads to exploitation. Just because a pharma brand can send a dopamine-triggering message doesn't mean it should. Just because it can suggest a lifestyle change at a moment of weakness doesn't mean it won't be coercive.

So the new marketers in pharma aren't just storytellers.

They're stewards.

Of privacy.

Of dignity.

Of choice.

Because a brand that nudges too hard becomes a brand that manipulates.

And a story that forgets its ethics becomes a fable without a moral.

Human First, Data Second

Let's return to George.

What if, instead of that bland algorithmic message, his smartwatch buzzed softly and said:

"Hi George. We noticed a few signs of stress this week. Just checking in. If you'd like, we can connect you with someone to talk to. Or just share a story from someone who's been through something similar."

Now that is wearable-enabled pharma marketing with a soul.

It's not just personal.

It's not just predictive.

It's profound.

It acknowledges that George is not a data point. He's a person with a pulse and a past.

The Takeaway

Pharma marketing in the wearable age will be one of the greatest storytelling opportunities—and responsibilities—of our time.

It will tempt us with precision.

But it must be guided by compassion.

It will dazzle with data.

But must remain rooted in human stories.

It will empower.

But must never overpower.

Because in the end, the future won't belong to the brands with the smartest algorithms.

It will belong to those with the deepest understanding of what it means to be human.

APPENDICES

Appendix A: Glossary of Wearable Tech Terms

Appendix B: Timeline of Major Wearable Milestones

Appendix C: Annotated Bibliography and Research References

Appendix D: Pharma-Wearable Alliance Tracker

Appendix E: Regulatory Landscape Snapshot

Appendix F: The Wearable-Ready Brand Manager: Self-Assessment Checklist

Appendix G: Three Case Studies

Appendix A

Glossary of Wearable Tech Terms

A quick-reference guide for pharma professionals navigating the evolving landscape of wearable technologies.

A

Affective Computing

A field of study that enables devices to recognize, interpret, and respond to human emotions using physiological signals like heart rate, facial expressions, and voice tone.

AI (Artificial Intelligence)

Computational systems that simulate human intelligence, used in wearables for predictive analytics, anomaly detection, behavioral triggers, and personalization.

Algorithmic Nudging

The use of data-driven prompts—based on biometric or behavioral inputs—to influence user actions or decisions, such as medication adherence reminders.

B

Biosensor

A device that detects and transmits information about a biological state (e.g., glucose level, ECG, temperature, motion). Core to most wearables.

Biometric Data

Physiological data collected from wearables, such as heart rate, oxygen saturation, respiration rate, skin temperature, or movement.

Bluetooth Low Energy (BLE)

A short-range wireless protocol optimized for energy-efficient data transfer between wearable devices and smartphones.

C

CGM (Continuous Glucose Monitoring)

A wearable technology that tracks glucose levels in real time, often used in diabetes management and pharma clinical trials.

Companion Wearable

A wearable device paired with a drug to monitor efficacy, side effects, or adherence. Often used in beyond-the-pill strategies.

Cyber-Physical Systems

Integrated systems where physical components (wearables) are closely linked with software and data analytics in real-time.

D

Data Integration

The merging of wearable-collected data with EHRs, pharma CRMs, or cloud-based analytics platforms to form a unified patient or consumer profile.

Digital Biomarker

A quantifiable physiological or behavioral data point collected via a digital device, used as a surrogate for health outcomes or disease progression.

Digital Therapeutics (DTx)

Evidence-based software-driven interventions that use wearables and apps to prevent, manage, or treat diseases.

E

ECG (Electrocardiogram)

A biometric signal measuring the electrical activity of the heart; available in advanced wearables like Apple Watch and used in cardiac trials.

Edge Computing

The processing of data directly on wearable devices (or nearby), reducing the need to send information to distant servers—improves speed and privacy.

F

Form Factor

The physical shape and design of a wearable device—watch, patch, ring, implant—that affects usability, comfort, and adoption.

G

GPS (Global Positioning System)

Used in wearables to track movement, location-based behavior, or lifestyle patterns relevant to disease monitoring or patient segmentation.

H

HRV (Heart Rate Variability)

A measure of the variation in time between heartbeats—used as a marker of stress, fatigue, and autonomic nervous system activity.

I

Implantable Wearables

Miniature medical devices embedded within the body that continuously monitor physiological data (e.g., cardiac rhythm).

Interoperability

The ability of different wearables, platforms, and pharma systems to exchange, interpret, and use data cohesively.

M

mHealth (Mobile Health)

A broad term for using mobile and wireless technologies (including wearables) in healthcare delivery and pharma engagement.

N

N-of-1 Trial

A clinical research design using a single patient, often empowered by wearable data, to evaluate the effectiveness of an intervention.

P

PGHD (Patient-Generated Health Data)

Health-related data created by patients through wearables or mobile apps, outside of traditional clinical encounters.

Pill+ Platform

A combination of ingestible sensors and medications (e.g., Abilify MyCite) that allows tracking of ingestion, timing, and adherence.

R

Remote Monitoring

The use of wearables to track patient data in real time from a distance, used in clinical trials and chronic disease management.

S

Smart Patch

A skin-adhering wearable used to collect biometric data (e.g., temperature, sweat, EEG), often disposable and low-profile.

Smartwatch

A wrist-worn device capable of displaying information, tracking biometric data, and interacting with apps. Common in trials and DTx.

T

Telemedicine Integration

Wearable data used to supplement remote consultations, enhancing diagnosis, disease tracking, and engagement.

Touchwear

A term describing wearables as active brand interfaces, integrating pharma engagement into the patient's physical experience.

U

UX (User Experience) Design

The overall usability, design, and emotional resonance of wearable tech. Critical for adoption and long-term behavior change.

V

Voice Biomarker

Data derived from vocal patterns that can indicate disease states (e.g., Parkinson's, depression), increasingly explored via wearables.

W

Wearable Ecosystem

An integrated system of wearable devices, software platforms, pharma data pipelines, and stakeholder interactions.

WearComp

An early wearable computing platform developed by Steve Mann in the 1980s, considered the origin of modern wearables.

Appendix B

Timeline of Major Wearable Milestones

A Chronology of Innovation, From Eyepieces to Ingestibles

1286 – The Invention of Eyeglasses

The very first wearable technology. Crafted in Italy, these vision-correcting lenses mark the beginning of augmenting the human body through external devices.

1665 – Christiaan Huygens and the Wearable Timekeeper

The Dutch scientist improves the accuracy of pendulum clocks, inspiring later versions of personal, wearable timekeeping devices.

1900s – Hearing Aids Become Portable

From bulky tabletop devices to wearable units powered by batteries, hearing aids become one of the first widespread medical wearables.

1961 – Edward O. Thorp and Claude Shannon's Roulette Wearable

The MIT mathematicians develop the first wearable computer: a shoe-concealed device to predict roulette wheel outcomes—an early fusion of sensors and strategy.

1980s – Steve Mann and the "WearComp"

Often considered the father of wearable computing, Mann creates a head-mounted display and body-worn computer, anticipating AR, lifelogging, and connected clothing.

1998 – Polar Introduces Wearable Heart Rate Monitor for Athletes

The launch of mainstream biometric tracking, ushering wearables into the fitness world and soon after, into clinical and wellness domains.

2002 – SenseCam Prototype by Microsoft Research

A pendant camera that auto-records images based on motion and light changes. This early lifelogging device lays groundwork for passive health monitoring.

2009 – Fitbit Launches First Step Tracker

The Fitbit Classic tracks steps and calories, revolutionizing consumer health behavior and introducing gamified wellness into everyday life.

2011 – Dexcom's Real-Time CGM Wins FDA Approval

Dexcom becomes a major player in continuous glucose monitoring (CGM), enabling real-time diabetes management and transforming chronic care delivery.

2013 – Google Glass Unveiled

Though commercially short-lived, Glass introduces augmented reality wearables into public discourse, influencing future iterations in surgery and pharma training.

2014 – Apple Watch Announced

Apple's flagship wearable goes beyond fitness to include heart rate, ECG (later), and app integrations. This catalyzes the consumerization of medical-grade features.

2015 – Propeller Health Partners with GSK

A pioneering digital health collaboration to use inhaler-attached sensors for asthma and COPD—one of pharma's first major wearables partnerships.

2016 – Novartis + Proteus Digital Health Collaborate on Digital Pills

Launch of ingestible sensor-equipped medications (like Abilify MyCite) to track adherence—marking a new frontier: drug-device convergence.

2017 – FDA Approves Apple Watch EKG Feature

Apple Watch becomes the first over-the-counter consumer device with FDA-cleared ECG, signaling regulatory openness to hybrid consumer-clinical tech.

2018 – AiCure Uses AI Facial Recognition to Monitor Pill Ingestion

A novel approach to adherence tracking using computer vision via smartphone camera—no wearable, but fully wearable-adjacent and pivotal to pharma trials.

2020 – Roche + Apple Collaborate on Parkinson's Monitoring

Smartwatch-based tremor and gait tracking integrated into clinical studies, offering passive, real-world data to improve trial outcomes and endpoints.

2020 – COVID-19 Accelerates Remote Monitoring

Wearables become essential tools in tracking symptoms, vitals, and vaccine effects—pharma embraces decentralized trials and virtual endpoints.

2021 – Fitbit Partners with Boehringer Ingelheim and Bristol-Myers Squibb

Focus on atrial fibrillation detection, early screening, and behavior change interventions—wearables enter preventive cardiology marketing.

2022 – Takeda Uses Wearables in Oncology Trials

Wearable patches and biosensors track fatigue, HRV, and pain in real time—redefining subjective endpoints in cancer research.

2023 – Launch of Apple's ResearchKit-Powered Health Studies

Millions of users contribute real-time data to health studies, in collaboration with pharma and research institutions—crowdsourced, wearable-based clinical research is born.

2024 – Rise of Smart Skin Patches and Implantables

Flexible biosensor wearables evolve to track hydration, pH, cytokines, and electrolytes—opening new windows into drug response and patient well-being.

2025 – Pharma Begins Building Wearable Ecosystems

From apps and patches to digital twins and smart packaging, pharma brand managers begin embedding wearables across the entire patient journey.

Appendix C

Annotated Bibliography and Research References

A Curated Guide to the Foundations and Frontiers of Wearable Technologies in Pharma

This annotated bibliography offers a carefully selected collection of academic papers, industry reports, books, and landmark studies that informed the insights in this book. Each entry includes a brief annotation explaining its relevance to the wearable revolution in pharmaceutical marketing, clinical trials, patient engagement, and digital health ethics.

1. **Picard, R. W. (1997). Affective Computing. MIT Press.**

   The foundational text that launched the field of emotional AI. Rosalind Picard's work is essential for understanding how wearables can detect and respond to physiological signals like stress and emotion—critical for behavior-modifying therapeutics and personalized pharma campaigns.

2. **Mann, S. (2013). Wearable Computing. Springer.**

   Steve Mann, the father of wearable tech, explores the evolution from body-worn cameras to augmented memory and sensor-enhanced reality. His theories directly inspire how pharma can embed itself in real-time, lived experiences.

3. **Swan, M. (2012). The Quantified Self: Fundamental Disruption in Big Data Science and Biological Discovery. Big Data, 1(2), 85-99.**

   A key academic paper that laid out the promise of self-tracking as a new epistemology. It supports arguments for PGHD (Patient-Generated Health Data) as clinical-grade evidence.

4. **Topol, E. (2015). The Patient Will See You Now: The Future of Medicine is in Your Hands. Basic Books.**

   A provocative look at how digital health—especially mobile and wearable tech—is shifting power from doctor to patient. A must-read for pharma brand managers rethinking patient empowerment.

5. **AiCure. (2020). Clinical Validation of AI-Based Visual Monitoring for Medication Adherence. White Paper.**

   Provides clinical trial data showing increased adherence through AI-driven facial recognition—highlighting a real-world example of digital behavioral nudging in pharma.

6. **FDA (2021). Digital Health Innovation Action Plan. U.S. Food and Drug Administration.**

   A foundational regulatory document outlining the FDA's evolving position on digital health, wearables, and Software-as-a-Medical-Device (SaMD). Crucial for pharma legal and compliance teams.

7. **Deloitte (2022). Connected Health: How Digital Technologies Are Transforming Pharma. Deloitte Insights.**

   This industry report maps how wearables, AI, and IoT are reshaping pharma—from R&D to commercialization. Offers market data and case studies cited in Chapters 5–11.

8. **GSK + Propeller Health. (2016). Results from Digital Inhaler Adherence Pilot. Industry Case Study.**

   Details the partnership's outcomes in asthma management—one of the first successful examples of pharma + wearable convergence to improve health outcomes.

9. **Novartis + Proteus Digital Health. (2018). Digital Medicines Study: Aripiprazole MyCite and Schizophrenia Adherence. Internal Data Report.**

   Although not peer-reviewed, this internal study (partially public via investor communications) offers lessons in drug-device integration and market readiness challenges.

10. **Roche + Apple. (2020). Smartwatch-Based Parkinson's Disease Monitoring Pilot. Research Collaboration Brief.**

Summarizes Roche's clinical exploration of passive monitoring via Apple Watch—supporting the use of wearables for continuous endpoints in neurodegenerative disease trials.

11. **Open mHealth. (2021). Building an Interoperable Wearable Health Ecosystem. Technical Brief.**

A foundational reference on creating device-agnostic data standards for wearable tech—helpful for brand teams looking to integrate across platforms.

12. **WHO (2021). Ethics and Governance of Artificial Intelligence for Health. World Health Organization.**

Addresses data privacy, algorithmic bias, and human oversight—key issues when pharma engages with AI-powered wearables.

13. **IBM Watson Health + Mayo Clinic. (2021). AI-Augmented Diagnosis and Wearable Data Integration. Case Study Summary.**

Offers real-world insight into the early convergence of enterprise AI, biosensor data, and clinical workflows—an emerging blueprint for pharma partnerships.

14. **HIMSS (2023). State of Interoperability in Digital Health. Industry Survey Report.**

Explores challenges and advances in making wearable data flow freely across platforms—useful for regulatory, IT, and marketing teams alike.

15. **European Medicines Agency (EMA). (2022). Use of Wearables in Clinical Trials: Qualification Opinion.**

The EMA's position paper clarifying how wearable-derived endpoints can be validated for use in drug development—relevant for global trial planning.

Appendix D

Pharma–Wearable Alliance Tracker

Mapping the Landscape of Collaborations Shaping the Future of Pharma

This appendix offers a curated tracker of notable partnerships between pharmaceutical companies and wearable technology firms. These alliances reflect the shifting paradigm—where pills are no longer enough, and the future lies in platforms, sensors, and continuous engagement.

The following entries are organized chronologically and categorized by the primary objective of the collaboration: clinical trials, digital therapeutics, adherence, real-world evidence, or brand engagement.

1. **Roche + Apple**

   Focus: Clinical Trial Endpoint Monitoring (Parkinson's)

   Year: 2019–present

   Details: Roche partnered with Apple to passively monitor tremors and gait changes in Parkinson's disease patients via the Apple Watch. Enabled continuous, real-world measurement of motor symptoms outside the clinic.

2. **Otsuka + Proteus Digital Health**

   Focus: Digital Medicine + Adherence (Schizophrenia)

   Year: 2017–2020

   Details: FDA-approved Abilify MyCite—an antipsychotic embedded with an ingestible sensor. The pill transmitted ingestion confirmation to a wearable patch and smartphone. Discontinued due to cost, privacy concerns, and low uptake.

3. **GSK + Propeller Health**

   Focus: Inhaler Adherence + Asthma Management

   Year: 2015–2018

Details: Propeller's smart inhalers captured usage data and nudged patients to improve adherence. GSK integrated insights into asthma drug programs. The success helped drive digital inhalers into mainstream awareness.

4. **Pfizer + Fitbit**

   Focus: Atrial Fibrillation Research + Early Detection

   Year: 2020

   Details: Pfizer teamed up with Fitbit (later acquired by Google) to explore wearable detection of irregular heart rhythms. The goal was early diagnosis and linkage to therapeutic interventions.

5. **Biogen + Apple**

   Focus: Cognitive Health + Early Alzheimer's Detection

   Year: 2021–Present

   Details: Joint research initiative to use Apple Watch and iPhone to identify early signs of cognitive decline. If successful, may reshape how Alzheimer's drugs are deployed and monitored.

6. **Dexcom + Eli Lilly**

   Focus: Closed-Loop Diabetes Care

   Year: 2019–present

   Details: Integration of Dexcom's Continuous Glucose Monitors with Lilly's smart insulin pen for a real-time, adaptive diabetes management ecosystem.

7. **Boehringer Ingelheim + Fitbit**

   Focus: COPD Disease Awareness Campaign

   Year: 2018

   Details: Leveraged Fitbit data to promote awareness of movement limitations in COPD. Bridged marketing with public health in a novel way.

8. **Takeda + Empatica**

   Focus: Oncology Trial Monitoring

   Year: 2022–Present

   Details: Wearable biosensors from Empatica monitor fatigue, pain, HRV, and sleep in cancer patients—offering digital biomarkers for subjective endpoints in trials.

9. **AiCure + Multiple Sponsors (including Novartis)**

   Focus: AI-Based Visual Adherence

   Year: 2016–Present

   Details: Uses smartphone AI and facial recognition to confirm pill ingestion. Deployed in CNS and infectious disease trials. Boosted adherence by 18% in pilot studies.

10. **Sanofi + BioIntelliSense**

   Focus: Remote Monitoring + COVID Therapeutic Trials

   Year: 2021

   Details: Integrated BioSticker wearable sensors to collect real-time data on patient vitals during COVID-19 therapeutic trials. Facilitated remote trial management.

11. **Novartis + SmartSensor Telehealth Projects**

   Focus: Heart Failure + Readmission Prevention

   Year: 2020–present

   Details: Piloted wearable sensors for heart failure patients to track fluid retention, helping to predict exacerbations and reduce hospital readmissions.

12. **Bayer + One Drop**

   Focus: Digital Therapeutic Integration (Diabetes)

   Year: 2020

   Details: Bayer invested $98M in One Drop to co-develop data-driven diabetes care plans with wearables and AI-based coaching.

13. **Merck + Evidation Health**

   Focus: Behavioral Data + Health Incentives

   Year: 2019

   Details: Collaboration to gather patient-reported outcomes and behavior data from wearables to inform clinical insights, while incentivizing health behavior through rewards.

Tracking Themes Emerging from These Alliances:

A. **From Trials to Treatments**: Wearables are no longer just data-gathering tools; they are therapeutic and diagnostic enablers.

B. **Closed-Loop Ecosystems**: CGM + smart pens, smart pills + apps—integrations are becoming end-to-end ecosystems.

C. **AI-Powered Adherence**: Facial recognition, reminders, nudges, and predictive alerts are now standard features.

D. **Marketing Meets Monitoring**: Wearables help reposition brands as health partners, not just pill providers.

E. **Privacy-Performance Tension**: The most innovative alliances also test the limits of data governance and ethical design.

Appendix E

Regulatory Landscape Snapshot

How Global Agencies are Shaping the Future of Wearables in Pharma?

The intersection of wearable technology and pharmaceutical innovation has outpaced traditional regulatory frameworks. This appendix offers a concise yet comprehensive snapshot of how leading global regulators—FDA (United States), EMA (European Union), MHRA (UK), PMDA (Japan), and WHO—are adapting to the wearable era. The focus is on clinical validation, real-world evidence, patient safety, data privacy, and Software-as-a-Medical-Device (SaMD).

United States: Food and Drug Administration (FDA)

1. **Digital Health Innovation Action Plan (2017)**

   A landmark move that laid the foundation for regulating digital health technologies, including wearables. It introduced the concept of a pre-certification program for software developers, focusing on organizational excellence rather than product-by-product review.

2. **Software as a Medical Device (SaMD) Framework**

   Developed in collaboration with the International Medical Device Regulators Forum (IMDRF), the FDA recognizes wearable devices that provide diagnostic or therapeutic functions as SaMD, requiring a risk-based review.

3. **Real-World Evidence (RWE) Program**

   Wearable-derived data is now considered a valid source of clinical evidence under certain conditions, especially for post-market surveillance and supplemental indications.

4. **21st Century Cures Act (2016)**

   Encouraged the use of patient-generated health data (PGHD)—such as that from wearable devices—in clinical decision-making and research.

   Key Implication for Pharma: The FDA is encouraging innovation but expects transparency, audit trails, and data integrity in wearable-derived evidence.

European Union: European Medicines Agency (EMA)

1. **Qualification Opinion on Digital Endpoints (2022)**

   Issued a positive scientific opinion on using wearable-derived endpoints (e.g., gait speed, activity levels) in Parkinson's and other neurodegenerative disease trials.

2. **GDPR (General Data Protection Regulation)**

   Enforces stringent consent, purpose limitation, and data minimization rules—particularly challenging when pharma engages with wearable companies collecting continuous biosignals.

3. **AI Regulation Draft (2021-2024)**

   Proposed legislation that treats emotion-recognition and biometric classification as high-risk applications. This will impact biosignal-triggered marketing and nudges via wearables.

   Key Implication for Pharma: The EMA encourages the use of digital endpoints but demands rigorous ethical standards and full data anonymization in all wearable device deployments.

United Kingdom: MHRA (Medicines and Healthcare Products Regulatory Agency)

1. **Post-Brexit Regulatory Autonomy**

   MHRA now operates independently of the EMA, creating its own "Innovative Devices Access Pathway" which includes wearable technologies.

2. **Early Engagement Initiatives**

   Encourages pharma and med-tech companies to seek early advice on digital tools, especially for oncology, neurology, and rare disease applications.

   Key Implication for Pharma: MHRA is fast-tracking wearables in trials but emphasizes patient safety, clear benefit-risk analysis, and interoperability.

Japan: PMDA (Pharmaceuticals and Medical Devices Agency)

1. **Harmonization with FDA/EMA**

   Japan follows many global standards (like SaMD definitions), but has more conservative adoption timelines.

2. **Use of Wearables in Remote Trials**

   Endorses remote monitoring technologies in post-approval studies and long-term safety surveillance, particularly during the COVID-19 period.

Key Implication for Pharma: Japan is cautiously supportive, especially in geriatrics and chronic disease tracking, but expects local validation.

World Health Organization (WHO)

1. **Ethics and Governance of Artificial Intelligence for Health (2021)**

   Set global principles for AI, wearables, and digital health tools: including transparency, inclusiveness, explainability, and human oversight.

2. **Digital Health Atlas & Interoperability Standards**

   Promotes country-level adoption of common data standards to enable wearable integration into national health systems, particularly in low- and middle-income countries.

Key Implication for Pharma: WHO offers a framework for equitable use of wearables in global health and encourages responsible partnerships.

Cross-Cutting Themes Pharma Must Navigate

Regulatory Change	Impact on Pharma-Wearable Integration
Classification as Medical Devices or SaMD	Determines need for regulatory filings, trials, or labeling
Data Privacy & Consent	Varies by region (e.g., GDPR, HIPAA) and governs how pharma can use wearable data
Validation of Digital Endpoints	Pharma must justify sensor accuracy, algorithm logic, and clinical relevance
Equity & Access Concerns	Regulators want evidence that wearables won't worsen the digital divide
Interoperability Standards	Pharma encouraged to align with HL7 FHIR, OpenmHealth, etc.

Closing Note:

The regulatory landscape is evolving—but not always in sync with the pace of innovation. For pharma marketers, clinical teams, and digital strategists, proactive regulatory engagement is no longer optional—it is a competitive advantage.

Appendix F

The Wearable-Ready Brand Manager: Self-Assessment Checklist

Introduction

As pharmaceutical marketing enters the age of connected health, brand managers must evolve beyond traditional playbooks. Wearable technologies offer real-time, biometric, and behavioral data that demand new thinking, new tools, and new responsibilities. This self-assessment checklist is designed to help you gauge your readiness, identify gaps, and spark strategic alignment for the wearable age.

Section 1: Strategic Mindset

1.1 Patient-Centered Thinking:

- Have I shifted from a product-centered model to a patient-journey-first approach?
- Do I actively seek out patient needs that wearables can address (e.g., adherence, symptom tracking, lifestyle triggers)?

1.2 Ecosystem Awareness:

- Am I aware of the major players in the wearable health space (Apple, Fitbit, Dexcom, Oura, etc.)?
- Have I explored existing pharma-wearable partnerships and their outcomes?

1.3 Opportunity Mapping:

- Can I identify where wearables intersect with my therapeutic area (e.g., neurology, cardiology, oncology)?
- Have I mapped biometric opportunities across awareness, engagement, adherence, and outcomes?

Section 2: Data Fluency

2.1 Understanding Biosignals:

- Do I understand the basics of what wearables measure (e.g., HRV, SpO_2, ECG, sleep patterns)?
- Can I interpret these in the context of disease progression or patient behavior?

2.2 Real-Time Thinking:

- Am I comfortable thinking in real-time data cycles, not just quarterly metrics?
- Can I envision messaging strategies triggered by biometric events?

2.3 Privacy & Compliance:

- Am I familiar with the ethical and legal implications of biometric data use (GDPR, HIPAA, 21st Century Cures Act)?
- Do I have clear guardrails in place for consent, anonymization, and data ownership?

Section 3: Cross-Functional Collaboration

3.1 Working with Data Scientists:

- Have I partnered with analytics teams to develop AI/ML-driven insights from wearable data?
- Do I understand how to translate raw data into segmentation, personalization, and content recommendations?

3.2 Engaging with Regulatory and Legal:

- Have I involved compliance teams early when developing wearable-enabled campaigns or programs?
- Do I understand how wearable-linked evidence may impact claims, submissions, or pharmacovigilance?

3.3 Partnering with Platforms:

- Have I explored partnerships with tech companies or startups in the wearable space?
- Do I have a framework for evaluating wearable platforms (interoperability, adoption, clinical validation)?

Section 4: Campaign & Experience Design

4.1 Contextual Messaging:

- Can I build messaging frameworks that respond to biometric triggers (e.g., elevated heart rate, disrupted sleep)?
- Do I have content modularity ready for such hyper-personalized experiences?

4.2 Journey Mapping & UX:

- Have I reimagined the patient journey map in light of real-time wearable data?
- Are my brand's touchpoints designed to feel helpful, timely, and humane?

4.3 Measurement & ROI:

- Do I have KPIs beyond awareness—like engagement per biometric state, behavior change, or adherence uplift?
- Can I track the downstream impact of wearable-linked campaigns on clinical and commercial outcomes?

Scoring Your Readiness

- 16–20 "Yes" Answers: You're not just ready — you're leading. Consider publishing your approach or mentoring others.
- 10–15 "Yes" Answers: Strong footing. Time to prioritize a few key gaps and pilot a wearable-enabled campaign.
- 5–9 "Yes" Answers: Early stage. Engage with case studies, cross-functional partners, and vendors to accelerate your learning.
- 0–4 "Yes" Answers: The wearable wave is coming fast. Begin with foundational education and external landscape scanning.

Final Thought

In a world where biosignals are communication channels and adherence is a behavioral journey, your role as a brand manager is no longer just to inform—it's to anticipate, respond, and resonate. This checklist is your compass. The path ahead is dynamic, but deeply human.

Appendix G

Three Case Studies

Case Study 1: The Beat Beneath the Glass: How a Watch Learned to Listen to the Heart?

On the face of it, it was just a watch. But inside, it was a bet—on silicon, on signal, on trust.

Somewhere in Cupertino, in a windowless lab behind layers of biometric security, an Apple engineer named Eugene Kim was watching heartbeats. Hundreds of them. Thousands, even. Not figuratively, but literally—waveforms streaming in real-time across giant monitors, like digital ocean tides. Each peak and valley represented a life in motion, a rhythm that could go wrong in the blink of an eye.

Back in 2013, Apple wasn't in the health business. It was in the business of delight—of creating devices that clicked and swiped, making life easier. But somewhere along the road to iPhones and AirPods, a curious shift began. People weren't just using Apple devices to text or stream music. They were using them to count steps. To track sleep. To log fertility. The body had become a platform—and Apple, quietly, was building the next operating system for health.

Enter the ECG project.

It started with a question: Could a wristwatch detect atrial fibrillation, the world's most common and most silent heart arrhythmia? The answer, technically, was yes. But technically wasn't good enough. Because this wasn't about tech. It was about trust. Could people—and regulators—trust a commercial gadget to do something once reserved for hospital-grade machines and white-coated cardiologists?

Apple did something radical. It didn't just double down on sensors. It tripled down on collaboration.

First, it drew in cardiologists—such as Dr. Sumbul Desai from Stanford—who helped calibrate the distinction between a false positive and a life-saving alert. Then it engaged hardware engineers who reimagined the Digital Crown not as a scroll wheel, but as a live electrode. Meanwhile, regulatory strategists worked hand-in-hand with the FDA—navigating approval processes typically reserved for medical device manufacturers, not consumer tech firms. Designers, too, had a seat at the table. They asked: How do you notify someone they may be in atrial fibrillation—without panicking them?

The answer wasn't a beep. It was a gentle tap. A haptic whisper on the wrist. Because fear wasn't the goal—awareness was.

In 2018, the Apple Watch Series 4 launched with an FDA-cleared ECG feature—a medical first. On stage, Apple's COO Jeff Williams said, "It's not just technology. It's the beginning of a new era in health."

He was right. Days after launch, news reports poured in: a man in Missouri who went to the ER because of an alert—and discovered he was in afib. A woman in Maine whose watch called out an irregular rhythm before her doctor could. The stories weren't marketing. They were validation. The Apple Watch had done something few in pharma had yet dared: it had become a therapeutic ally, not just a lifestyle gadget.

But perhaps the most powerful part of the story isn't the technology. It's the interdisciplinary symphony behind it. Engineers didn't just build. Doctors didn't just advise. Designers didn't just style. They all listened—to each other, and to the body. And in doing so, they made the invisible… visible.

The Apple Watch's ECG wasn't just an innovation. It was a signal—to pharma, to medtech, to marketing, to the world. That when technology listens deeply, the heart speaks.

Case Study 2: The Mind Map: How Verily and Behavioral Scientists Tried to Predict Emotion?

The question was almost too big to ask out loud:

Can we detect depression before a person even knows they're depressed?

Inside the white-walled campus of Verily, Alphabet's health moonshot subsidiary, the question was being asked quietly but insistently. Not by one person, but by a coalition of psychologists, machine learning engineers, behavioral economists, and former pharma researchers. The tools were not stethoscopes or scales, but wearables, keystrokes, gait patterns, and voice tone analysis. The mission? To turn behavior into a biomarker.

It started with a man named Dr. Thomas Insel. Former director of the National Institute of Mental Health, Insel had seen the numbers: over 280 million people globally living with depression; most undiagnosed until too late. "We wait for people to get sick enough to ask for help," he said. "What if we could see the signals before they suffer?"

That question found its way to Verily—where Project Baseline, originally a longitudinal study of health, became a sandbox for far more nuanced explorations.

Here's where the story gets… weird. But in a good way.

Instead of starting with drugs, Verily started with data traces—your sleep rhythms, typing speed, voice inflection, even how often you smile in selfies. Behavioral scientists began to build "emotion maps," not through therapy sessions, but through patterns—non-linear, high-frequency, cross-platform behaviors that whispered subtle shifts in mental state.

A lag in your typing speed? Might be fatigue.

A change in your walking cadence? Could signal anxiety.

A decline in how often you glance at your phone? Potential withdrawal.

These weren't diagnostic tools. Yet. But they were clues. And in a field like mental health, clues are everything.

Verily didn't go it alone. They partnered with behavioral health clinics, academic psychiatry departments, and even health insurers. And unlike many health-tech efforts that hit privacy walls, Verily made ethics part of the architecture. Participants opted in. Feedback was real-time. Patients weren't studied—they were empowered.

Then came a twist.

In one pilot, a group of patients with bipolar disorder were given a smartwatch tied to a real-time alert system. The device didn't just track sleep or HRV. It integrated with their care team—flagging concerning behavioral patterns. One patient reported receiving a call from a clinician just as she was about to spiral. "It was like the watch knew before I did," she said.

It wasn't magic. It was multidisciplinary orchestration.

Engineers calibrated models using neural networks. Psychologists helped interpret the fuzzy boundaries between normal and not. Clinicians turned data into decisions. And patients—crucially—became co-pilots, not data points.

But the story didn't end there. Pharma companies started calling. Could they use the same models to screen trial participants? To track side effects invisibly? Could this be the companion diagnostic of mood?

The implications rippled out fast:

- From treatment to prevention.
- From episodic care to continuous insight.
- From subjective mood scales to objective behavioral biomarkers.

This wasn't a tipping point, but an invisible pivot, where health shifted from what people say… to what they do, and how they move through space and time.

The Verily story is still unfolding. There are critics, of course. Privacy hawks. Clinical purists. Skeptics. But somewhere between the pulse and the pattern, the body and the mind, a new kind of medicine is taking shape.

Not just personalized.

But predictive.

And not because of a genius breakthrough, but because of an unlikely alliance—engineers and therapists, coders and clinicians, data and dignity.

That's the real miracle. Not the watch. Not the algorithm. But the idea that when we listen—deeply enough, respectfully enough—the human body and mind will always speak.

We just have to be ready to hear them.

Case Study 3: The Pulse Point: How a Pharma Brand used Heartbeats to Trigger Hope?

In 2022, a leading global pharmaceutical company—let's call it NeuroCore Therapeutics—was preparing for the launch of its new migraine prevention drug, Nureleva. The molecule was promising. The clinical trials were strong. But the market? Saturated. The challenge wasn't just reaching neurologists—it was reaching patients before the pain did.

Somewhere in the company's digital transformation lab, a marketer named Amira Patel asked a deceptively simple question:

"What if we didn't wait for patients to reach out to us? What if their bodies told us when to help?"

The idea that followed would become one of the most innovative hyperpersonalized pharma marketing campaigns in recent memory—built not on focus groups or surveys, but on wearables, AI, and real-time biosignal orchestration.

Step 1: The Signal

Neuro Core partnered with a network of wearable device companies—Fitbit, Garmin, and even smart ring startups. Through opt-in programs, migraine-prone users were encouraged to sync their wearable data (sleep, heart rate variability, stress scores, environmental triggers like light exposure) with the NeuroConnect app—an AI-powered companion platform co-developed with a healthtech firm specializing in behavioral neurometrics.

The goal? To build personalized migraine risk models.

And the surprising insight?

For many patients, subtle physiological shifts—like a sustained drop in HRV or increased resting heart rate—often preceded migraine episodes by 12 to 24 hours. In other words, the body knew before the brain did.

Step 2: The Dashboard

Behind the scenes, NeuroCore's marketing and medical teams weren't flying blind. They were using a wearable-linked CRM system, layered with AI dashboards that assigned each user a "Migraine Onset Probability Score" (MOPS)—a dynamic, biosignal-informed index updated hourly.

But here's where it got brilliant: the dashboard didn't just passively watch. It triggered action.

When a user's MOPS crossed a certain threshold, the system would send:

- A push notification reminding them of lifestyle tactics (hydration, light avoidance, relaxation techniques),
- A wearable alert via gentle vibration,

- And—if the user was prescribed Nureleva—a hyperpersonalized prompt: "Now's the optimal time to take your prevention dose. Based on your unique profile, early intervention could make today a pain-free day."

Everything was timed to their biosignal window—right message, right moment, right heartbeat.

Step 3: The Conversion

The marketing team tracked not impressions, but intervention adherence rates. Within 6 months:

- Adherence to the recommended dosing schedule rose by 27%.
- Users who followed the alerts reported 1.8 fewer migraine days/month.
- Patient satisfaction scores hit all-time highs, with 78% saying: "This is the first time a pharma brand felt like it was helping me in real time."

And the bonus?

The brand equity of Nureleva skyrocketed—not because of its chemistry alone, but because it showed up when patients needed it most, without waiting to be asked.

Why this Mattered?

It wasn't just a campaign. It was a humanized algorithm, a body-aware brand, a pulse-triggered promise that pharma could be something more than a label on a blister pack. It could be a partner in your pocket. A whisper on your wrist. A silent, personalized shield.

It worked not because it was flashy. But because it was intimate, invisible, and intelligent.

This was the "tipping point of pharma personalization"—when marketing finally stopped shouting and started listening.

About the Author

Subba Rao Chaganti

He has a master's in business administration and over fifty-two years of experience in

Pharmaceutical marketing. His experience encompasses all facets of the industry, from sales and sales management to product management and overseeing overall marketing activities. He has experience in both domestic and international marketing, as well as within the Indian and multinational sectors.

He also taught a course on Advertising and Brand Management as an adjunct professor at Gitam Institute of Foreign Trade (now part of Gitam University) in Visakhapatnam for a few years and a course on Marketing as a visiting faculty member at Jawaharlal Nehru Technological University (JNTU) in Hyderabad.

He lives in Farmington, Connecticut, USA, and can be reached at: subbarao.chaganti@gmail.com.

Here is a list of his publications:

1. Pharmaceutical Marketing in India: Concepts, Cases, Strategy
2. Game Plans for Post-GATT Era: Action Agenda of the Indian Pharmaceutical Industry
3. Compete or Forfeit: Strategies for Sustainable Competitive Advantage in the Pharma Product Patents Era
4. Pharmaceutical Marketing in India for Today and Tomorrow - 25th Anniversary Edition
5. Bullseyes and Blunders: Lessons from 100 Cases in Pharma Marketing
6. Digital Pharma Marketing Playbook: Winning With the New Rules of Engagement

7. Cracking the Generics Code: Your Single-Source Success Manual for Winning in Multi-Source Product Markets
8. Reimagine Pharma Marketing: Make It Future-Proof!
9. Brand Positioning in Pharma
10. Transactional to Transformational Marketing in Pharma: The Science of Why and The Art of How
11. A to Z of Pharmaceutical Marketing: World's First and Only Encyclopedia in Two Volumes
12. The Synergy of Minds: Human+AI Orchestrating the Pharma Marketing Revolution
13. Design Thinking for Pharma
14. The Pharma Product Manager: Navigating the Digital Frontier
15. Sentiment Analysis for Pharma Marketers
16. Whispering to AI: Prompt Engineering for Pharma Brand Managers
17. Storytelling in Pharma Marketing
18. Beyond the Molecule: The Art and Science of Metaphors That Matter
19. The Voices Within: Your Body Speaks, When Your Organs Tell Their Own Stories
20. Pharma Archetypes: The Science of Meaningful Healthcare Marketing
21. Human Futures: Navigating the AI Revolution with Purpose and Agency
22. Breaking Through: A Business Novel (based on the theory of constraints)

www.ingramcontent.com/pod-product-compliance
Lightning Source LLC
Chambersburg PA
CBHW071415230926
51846CB00001B/93
9789347311307